What's Wrong with my Snake?

John Rossi D.V.M., M.A.
and Roxanne Rossi

The Herpetocultural Library

Advanced Vivarium Systems, Inc.

P.O. Box 6050, Mission Viejo, CA 92690

Library of Congress Cataloging-in-Publication Data

Rossi, John. 1955-
    What's Wrong with my Snake?/ John Rossi and Roxanne Rossi.
        p. cm.
    Includes bibliographical references and index.
    ISBN 1-882770-35-8
    1. Captive snakes--Diseases. 2. Captive snakes.   I. Rossi,
Roxanne. II. Title.
IN PROCESS
639.3' 96--dc20

                                      96-15432
                                          CIP

PRINTED IN SINGAPORE.

Cover photography by Jim Bridges, John Baker, and Debby Feild.
All photography by the authors unless indicated.
Graphic design and layout by Bridget M. Pilcher.

This book is dedicated to the late Dr. James Corcoran, who was an outstanding reptile veterinarian, snake keeper, and friend.

Acknowledgements

The authors wish to thank Steve Barten D.V. M., Roger Klingenberg D.V. M. and Don Swerida D.V. M. for their support and photographic contributions.

Contents

Introduction 1

Disease and the Captive Environment 3

Acquiring a Snake 9

Selection of Snakes 13

Handling Snakes for Examination or Treatment 17

Anorexia and Inappetance (Not Eating) 25

Maladaptation 31

Burns 33

Constipation 36

Dehydration 39

Dermatitis (Skin Lesions) 41

Diarrhea 45

Dysecdysis (Improper Shedding) 47

Egg Care 49

Escape (Management of) 53

Feeding Frequency and Obesity 57

Geriatrics 61

Identification 65

Medicines 67

Problem/Solution Chart I-II 69-70

Most Commonly Used Drugs in Snakes 71

Small Snake Antibiotic Chart I-III 72-74

Large Snake Antibiotic Chart 75

Deworming Chart 76

Overheating 77

Parasites 79

Pediatrics and the Pediatric
    Environment (Perinatology) 89

Personal Hygiene and Quarantine 94

Psychological Factors 99

Reproductive Failure/Dystocia 105

Respiratory Problems 113

Seizures, Tremors, Incoordination, and Symptoms of
    Neurological Problems 117

Stomatitis (Mouth Rot) 121

Sudden Death 124

Transportation 127

Trauma (Rodent Injuries, Escape Injuries) 131

Vomiting and Regurgitation 135

Weight Loss 139

Choosing a Veterinarian 143

Index 149

Introduction

Snakes are among the fastest growing groups of captive animals in the United States. Although once the object of loathing and fascination, snakes have become the focus of an increasing number of herpetoculturists: hobbyists involved in the captive maintenance and propagation of reptiles and amphibians.

The relatively recent popularity of snakes can be attributed to their streamlined and often striking geometric beauty, fascinating movement and interesting behaviors, ease of care and handling, and with many species a certain docility. As the number of snakes in captivity has increased, so has awareness of their requirements and medical problems. Veterinarians, confronted with a growing number of reptile patients, have made tremendous progress in the field of herpetological medicine over the past ten years. Although there are several technical references on the veterinary treatment of reptiles, there are few user-friendly home medical references dealing specifically with the common medical problems of snakes and their treatment. The authors have compiled this concise, easy-to-use manual in order to fill an important gap in the popular herpetocultural literature.

This book presents the medical problems of captive snakes based on the apparent signs of disease, stress, and inability to acclimate to captivity. These signs, their causes, and their treatments are discussed in this book. They are arranged alphabetically in order to facilitate ease of access. There also are sections on the problems of very young snakes, very old snakes, gravid or pregnant snakes, and escaped snakes, as well as emergency treatment for overheated snakes. Explanations for unusual behaviors and sudden deaths appear in the sections on psychological factors and sudden death. A medicine chart is included to help veterinarians dose snakes properly, in case they are inexperienced with these animals.

Above all this book has focused on prevention and presents the many aspects of husbandry that will help prevent the onset of problems before they become serious.

Disease and the
Captive Environment

Perhaps the most important concept in herpetoculture is
that of the relationship between disease and the captive
environment. If an animal is placed in a proper environment (either a natural one or a manmade re-creation of
essential aspects of the natural environment), disease is
unlikely to occur. In an artificial environment you can
reduce the likelihood of disease in reptiles in the following
ways: (1) cater to their immune system by keeping them
warm but with access to a thermal gradient; (2) reduce
stress by housing them singly and by not handling them;
(3) feed them a high-quality diet; and (4) control parasites
and maintain cleanliness.

With some species, however, you must come very
close to re-creating the natural environment or you will be
unsuccessful in your attempts to maintain them in captivity. Indeed, the degree to which we perceive certain snakes
as being difficult to keep in captivity is determined largely
by how well they accept artificial environments and diets.
We would regard as "easy" those snakes that require only
a standard thermal gradient, proper humidity, simple and
easily replaced substrate, and a hide box, while those
requiring a more complex re-creation of aspects of their
physical or biological environment we consider to be
"difficult." In both cases, the captive environment is

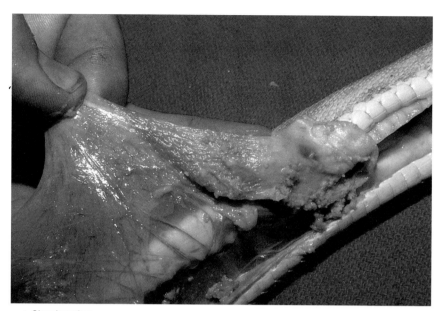

▲ *Chondropython necropsy showing severe pneumonia with chunks of pus.*

Photo by Don Swerida, D.V.M.

critical, and any successful treatment of disease in reptiles will involve correcting the environment *first*. Cowan (1980) and Ross and Marzec (1984) provide excellent discussions on the relationship of environment and disease. [Also, see the discussion in this book on *Psychological Factors*.]

DISEASE-PREVENTING ENCLOSURES AND PROCEDURES

It is impossible to generalize about the captive requirements of all 2,700 species of snakes. The specifics are not known for most species; however, there are certain basics that are considered to be important in the successful maintenance of those species studied to date. These basic requirements include the following.

Caging

Snakes are usually most safely housed indoors in smooth-sided, well-ventilated enclosures that have a perimeter larger than the length of the snake. Suitable caging materials include glass, plastic, and metal; all of these have smooth, nonporous surfaces and are easy to disinfect. Untreated wood is generally not suitable, because it is abrasive and is not easily disinfected. Treated lumber contains many toxic chemicals, which make it completely unsuitable for herpetoculture. Any enclosures used for keeping snakes should have an effective locking mechanism to prevent escape.

Substrate

The substrate (or bottom material) is a critical factor in snake maintenance. The most frequently used substrates for most snakes include artificial turf, newspaper, aspen shavings, pine shavings, and cypress mulch. Do *not* use cedar shavings; they contain aromatic compounds that may lead to respiratory problems. Under *no* circumstances should you use towels or rags, as they hold too much moisture and can cause bacterial infections. Smaller snakes commonly require one of the more natural substrates, which may be mixed with soil in order to provide a semimoist burrowing medium. [See Rossi, 1992 and 1995, *Snakes of the United States and Canada Vol. 1* and *Vol 2*, another book in the series published by Krieger, for a more detailed discussion on the care of small snakes.]

Shelters and Hide Boxes

Hiding places are important to a well-designed enclosure. Most snake keepers provide an inverted plastic box, referred to as a "hide box," for their snakes. It is where a well-adjusted snake will spend the majority of its time.

Avoid cardboard boxes and boxes made of untreated wood, as they have frequently been associated with shedding problems and/or skin infections.

There are now many commercial products on the market for snake-hiding areas. Those made of plastic or cork bark work extremely well. Some of the newer enclosure designs include a false floor, which creates a very large, dark hiding place. Some herpetoculturists have independently discovered the benefits of placing a hide box up high in a cage; this is better accepted by some snakes, increases floor space, and provides easier accessibility at cleaning time.

Humidity and Ventilation

Most snakes appear to do well if they are maintained in middle humidity ranges (40 to 70 percent); however, desert snakes typically require lower humidity, while rainforest species may require higher humidity. It is

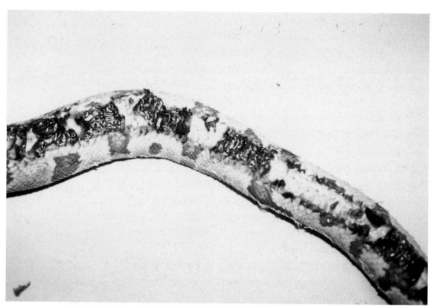

▲ *Belly scale burns in a boa constrictor.*
Photo by Don Swerida, D.V.M.

important that the proper humidity be maintained, but not at the expense of good ventilation. If cage ventilation is poor and the humidity is high, bacteria, mold, and fungi may grow rapidly and infect the snake. Thus, screen tops or numerous ventilation holes are necessary for most snake enclosures.

Thermal Gradient

Usually, a heat source is necessary for normal immune-system function and digestion in captive snakes. It also gives a psychological benefit by enabling a snake to thermoregulate freely. Heating pads or heat tapes are necessary equipment for captive snake maintenance. It is important to note that these heating devices need to be placed *outside* the cage. If you place these devices inside a cage, burns and and even electrocution may result. [See the section on burns.] Arboreal snakes may benefit tremendously from an overhead heat source, such as an incandescent bulb in a reflector-type fixture, which produces a warm spot among the branches in the cage. In any case, you should create a thermal gradient in the cage, with one localized warm spot and the rest of the cage cooler.

Lighting

To date, most snakes studied in captivity appear not to require ultraviolet (UV) light. Some snakes have been maintained and bred in captivity for many years with exposure to nothing more than filtered natural light. This may or may not be supplemented with artificial light, such as that produced by fluorescent or incandescent bulbs. There are anecdotal reports of appetite improvement in snakes exposed to full-spectrum fluorescent lights (Vita-Lite®, for example). We strongly encourage keepers of difficult snakes to experiment with supplemental full-spectrum fluorescent and/or incandescent lighting, to see if it will improve feeding and breeding success.

Diet

Researching your particular species' food preferences will be important in determining your feeding success with that species. Fortunately, most of the commonly maintained species will readily accept domestic mice as food, but some species may require food items that are difficult to procure. Such species are best left to the experts. You can train many species to accept a domestic rodent by rubbing a favored food item on it. This technique is called "scent transferring" and has been known to work extremely well; however, it is yet to be determined whether domestic rodents will represent a balanced long-term diet for snakes that normally eat other kinds of prey.

If a snake refuses rodents and must eat fish, the keeper must make every effort to provide whole fresh fish, or whole fresh fish that has recently been frozen and thawed. Be aware that diets made up solely of fish may predispose a captive snake to a thiamine deficiency with resultant neurological symptoms. This deficiency may be avoided either by feeding a varied diet or by supplementing the fish diet with a vitamin B1-containing supplement such as brewer's yeast. Dietary supplements are not normally necessary for snakes on a diet of whole rodents.

Cleaning and Disinfection

Although excessively frequent cleanings may create undue stress for some snakes, the benefits of cage cleanliness appear to outweigh the risks. Frequent removal of

It is strongly recommended you use bleach as a standard disinfectant.

▲ Children's Python (Liasis maculosus) in a filthy cage. Cage cleanliness and disinfection are critical to disease prevention. Bleach is an excellent and readily available disinfectant to use after eliminating the organic matter.

Photo by Steve Barten, D.V.M.

organic material and cage disinfection eliminate large numbers of pathogenic bacteria and break the life cycle of metazoan parasites that have direct life cycles. In other words, cage cleanliness is important.

You should remove organic material such as feces, shed skins, and uneaten animals as soon as you find them. This cleaning process is a necessary prerequisite to disinfection.

A wide variety of disinfectants have been recommended for use with reptiles. We think the most economical and effective disinfectant available is household bleach. Other disinfectants may have a broader spectrum of activity, but generally they are very toxic, are very expensive, or have an inadequate shelf life. These disinfectants are also more difficult to obtain. For these reasons, we strongly recommend bleach as a standard disinfectant. An effective dilution rate is 30 to 90 milliliters of bleach (1 to 3 ounces) per liter (quart) of water. This solution should be used at least once per month in the cage and once weekly to clean the water bowl. It may also be used for spot cleaning each time an animal defecates. [A more detailed discussion of disinfectants is presented in Rossi and Rossi, 1995.]

Acquiring a Snake

To the novice snake keeper, there may appear to be an endless array of snakes available for purchase in all different shapes, sizes, and colors. There are exotics and natives, melanistics and albinos, young and old, rare and common, expensive and cheap, males and females, captive-born and imported. How do you choose the best snake for you, and is there really a "best pet" snake?

With nearly 3,000 different kinds of snakes in existence, and literally hundreds of species presently available as pets, there is no one best captive snake. Many species appear to adapt readily to captivity and eat commonly available food items such as domestic rodents. Other species seem to adapt poorly to captivity and/or to require food items that are not readily available. It would seem logical, therefore, to choose a snake or snakes from the first group, unless you are very experienced in the maintenance of difficult snakes or have a great deal of time and money to invest in maintaining one of the more difficult species. After ease of maintenance, you should consider the following factors before making a decision.

The Adult Size of the Snake in Question

Careful consideration should be given to the adult size of the snake species you are selecting. For most people medium to large snakes are better choices than the giant snakes. Burmese pythons *(Python molurus bivittatus)* and green anacondas *(Eunectes murinus),* although cute when young, easily grow to more than ten feet in length within two years and ultimately reach more than 20 feet. Where will you house one of these snakes? Is it legal in your state to own such a large snake?

Disposition

What is the disposition of the species you are considering? Although disposition appears to be an individual trait, there are certain species that tend to be more aggressive than others. Arboreal boas *(Corallus)* have a reputation for aggression, and many of these snakes seem quite willing to bite their keepers.

Sex

In captivity female snakes are generally more aggressive feeders than males. The reason is unknown, but we suspect that it may be related to the higher food and energy demands that females must have for reproduction. Males have a lower risk of problems associated with reproduction.

Origin (Captive-born or Import)

The question will often arise of whether to purchase a captive-born or an imported snake. Imported animals are usually heavily parasitized and must be treated to remove these parasites; also, these animals may not adapt well to captivity. For these reasons, captive-born snakes are almost always preferable to wild-caught specimens. Selecting captive-bred snakes also reduces the demand for capture and importation of wild-caught snakes, thereby helping to preserve them in their natural habitat.

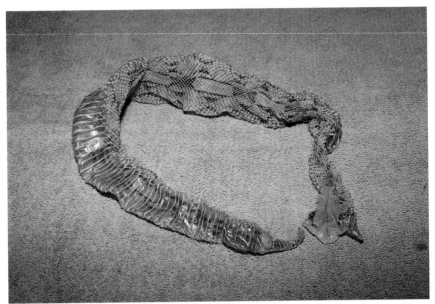

▲ The shed skin can tell quite a bit about a snake and its environment. This Gaboon viper skin reveals that the snake is in reasonably good health and the captive environment is okay, since the snake shed is in one piece. However, the discharge near the vent indicates that this snake has an anal gland abscess.

Age

A snake's age may be an important factor in deciding whether or not to acquire it. The young of some species—the gray-banded kingsnake *(Lampropeltis alterna)*, for example—are notoriously difficult to get started feeding; thus, many experts advise purchasing "well-started" juveniles or adults. Even though they may be more expensive, the difference in the ease of acclimation may be well worth the additional cost. On the other hand, with several species such as ball pythons, young animals are easier to acclimate than imported adults. Obtain information on the species you have selected to make the best decision at the time of purchase.

Appearance (color pattern)

The absolute very *last* characteristic to use in determining whether or not to purchase a snake as a pet is its appearance. A snake may be beautiful, but if it is very difficult to keep, very aggressive, or very large, it probably will be a source of grief to its owner, and thus will inevitably be much more likely to succumb in captivity. Thus, it is wise to resist the urge to purchase one of these animals purely on the basis of its appearance. The temperament of the animal and its health are far more important factors when making this important decision.

Selection of Snakes

COLUBRIDS

The larger, constricting, rodent-eating members of the colubrid family are among the most popular and easy to keep of all snakes. Popular and readily available species include kingsnakes, milk snakes, corn snakes, North American rat snakes, fox snakes, Trans Pecos rat snakes, Baird's rat snakes, pine snakes, and gopher snakes. In terms of docility, corn snakes are among the most recommended species, as are common kingsnakes.

Milksnakes are among the most beautiful of these snakes, but most species are too active for us to recommend them for handling. (Exceptions include Sinaloan and Andesian milksnakes.) North American rat snakes are hardy but will vary in their docility, depending upon subspecies and individual differences. Captive-raised black rat snakes and gray rat snakes are among the most docile, while Texas rat snakes may remain nippy even when raised in captivity. Fox snakes tend to be consistently docile but are somewhat more difficult to keep than other rat snakes. Gopher and pine snakes are commonly active when handled, but they tend to be docile and are among the most impressive and most underappreciated of the North American

▲ *Rough green snakes are among the more interesting snake species one can keep in captivity. They are attractive animals and display well in a properly designed vivarium.* Photo by Philippe de Vosjoli.

colubrids. Larger colubrid species, such as some of the rat snakes and the pine snakes, require more food and larger food items than some of the smaller species.

NATRICINE SNAKES

Natricine snakes, a subfamily of colubrids, include the popular garter snakes and the not-so-popular water snakes. Garter snakes are small attractive animals that can be maintained in correspondingly small enclosures and fed a diet of goldfish and supplemented fish fillet. Water snakes can be kept in a similar manner, but they are more likely to bite. We highly recommend these interesting snakes for beginners as well as the more experienced. An interest in selective breeding of rare morphs, such as albino checkered and Florida garter snakes and albino water snakes, has caused a renewed and fast-growing interest in this group of snakes.

▲ The corn snake is a relatively inexpensive snake that is tolerant of handling. However, excessive handling is stressful to most species of snakes.
Photo by Chris Wood.

BOIDS

Members of the boid family include some of the most popular and easy-to-maintain species. The following is an overview.

Species that remain relatively small: Rainbow boas, Rosy boas, sand boas, ball pythons, spotted pythons, green tree pythons. Ball pythons raised from hatchlings or yearlings are among the most highly recommended of pet snakes. They adapt well to captivity, do not grow to be too large, are relatively slow moving, and are easy to handle. They are also beautiful. Green tree pythons are recommended only for more experienced herpetoculturists. They are also more likely to bite than the other species mentioned.

Large species: Boa constrictors, West Indian boas (*Epicrates*), carpet pythons, and blood pythons. Of the large snakes, Colombian boa constrictors are the most recommended for those who want a large pet snake; they are typically docile and easy to care for.

Borneo blood pythons and carpet pythons raised from hatchlings tend to become docile.

Very large species: (At least two people are required to safely handle any of these animals as an adult.) Green anacondas, Asian rock pythons, African rock pythons, reticulated pythons, amethystine pythons, water pythons. Burmese pythons are among the most docile of all snakes. Statistically the two most dangerous species in captivity are the reticulated pythons and the African rock pythons. The main difficulty with these large species is that herpetoculturists use improper methods for feeding and handling them. On the other hand, some of the other very large species, such as anacondas, tend to be so aggressive that extra caution is invariably used when handling them, thus minimizing the risk of accidents and other problems.

The American Federation of Herpetoculturists has published guidelines for the keeping of large boas and pythons.The authors highly recommend that owners of the giant snakes obtain and follow these suggestions.

Handling Snakes for Examination or Treatment

When we handle snakes for pleasure, we generally exercise little or no restraint. Often, we allow a snake to glide freely over our hands or arms, and sometimes we allow it to wrap around an arm or leg. But the treatment of a snake for a medical problem or a close physical examination requires us to use restraint. You can restrain most small nonvenomous snakes by grasping them firmly but gently behind the head, near the angle of the jaws, and then supporting the body with your other hand.

Larger snakes generally require more support; five or more people may be needed to restrain a moderate-size snake for a physical examination or an injection. Large constrictors such as pythons, anacondas, and some boas are very powerful snakes; the uninformed novice may be unaware of just how dangerous they can be. As a general rule, you should handle *no* constricting snake of more than eight feet in length without someone else in the immediate vicinity. A thorough physical examination may require two people to hold such a snake while a third person examines the animal.

Caution: Because snakes and other reptiles have a single occipital condyle (only one part of the skull is in contact with the first neck vertebra), they are particularly susceptible to cervical dislocation: therefore, you must exercise extreme caution when handling snakes that struggle or twist vigorously.

A number of devices have been used to assist in the restraint of snakes for a physical examination or for other purposes. These include clear plexiglass tubes, foam rubber pads and plastic pressboard; even a snake bag or pillowcase can be used. If using a snake bag, you can keep one end of the snake in the bag while the other end is examined or injections are administered. Even though plastic tubes and foam rubber pads are commonly used for venomous snakes, they are also excellent for restraining aggressive or uncooperative nonvenomous snakes. The snake is maneuvered into the tube, after which the tube and the snake are grasped and held together.

If you are using a foam mat, gently place the snake upon the mat and then press the snake against the mat, using a clear shield. This procedure allows a careful examination, measurement, or treatment to be accomplished with some ease.

When administering an injection, be especially careful of sudden violent jerks by the snake toward the needle. We sometimes wrap our hands around the snake near the injection point in order to prevent or slow down this sudden jerking movement. This is also one of the main reasons that you should insert the needle at an angle, not perpendicular to the skin. If the needle is perpendicular, a sudden motion might cause it to penetrate too deeply, consequently causing serious harm to the snake.

Warning: Venomous snakes should *not* be handled, except as necessary for treatment. The two techniques mentioned here are also suitable for these animals.

Examining a Snake

To examine a snake, observe it from a distance at first, looking for overall appearance, ease of breathing, and luster of the skin. If it is moving about the cage, is it alert and moving with good muscular and motor control? Is its tongue flicking? Examine the cage for stools; are they solid and normal in color, or loose, watery, and foul smelling?

Normal snake stool should consist of a dark part (usually black or dark brown) and a white part. The dark part is the fecal matter (digested food and sloughed intestinal cells), and the white part is called uric acid. This is what most dry land reptiles produce instead of urea. Because uric acid is insoluble in water, it helps them

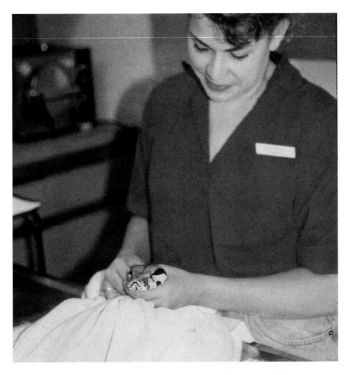

◄ This is an example of how to hold a larger snake, one hand is holding the head and the other hand holds the body firmly within a pillow case. This works well for snakes that tend to thrash or whip. Photo by Roger Klingenberg.

conserve body water. If the stool is excessively watery, mucusy, blood-tinged, greenish, or yellowish, it may signal a problem.

Ask to handle the snake (if it is nonvenomous). The body should feel strong and supple. As it crawls over your finger, hands, or arm, the snake's body in most cases should not noticeably flatten. If you detect flattening, it could indicate poor muscle tone and perhaps long-term anorexia.

Check the rostral (nose) area for abrasions, and then check the mouth. Hold the snake behind its head with one hand (while supporting the body on a table or using your arm to hold it against your body); with the other hand, gently pull the skin underneath the lower jaw to open the mouth of the animal. Is the mouth area clean, uniformly colored (usually pink, but it may be white or blue in some species), and free of excessive amounts of mucus? Look at the eyes. Are they bright, clear, and alertly moving to examine the environment? Once again, is the tongue

▲ *A ball python with rostral (nose) trauma. Cages with rough sides, low screen tops and no place to hide contribute to this problem.*

flicking? Check the nares (nostrils) and heat-sensing pits, if they are present. Are they clear of dried mucus plugs and parasites? Is the snake breathing easily, or are there respiratory "wheezes," open mouth breathing, puffing of the throat, blowing bubbles, or a constant head elevation?

Working from the head toward the tail, examine the skin. Are there any abnormalities or discolorations, especially ventrally? Are there any ticks or mites? Is the skin smooth and shiny (note: many species have keeled scales) or dry, abraded, and/or peeling? Are there any abnormal lumps or bumps?

Next, run your fingers gently along the abdomen of the snake. Do you feel any firm masses? Check the cloacal area. Is it clean with a pink interior, or is there dried blood or mucus present (sometimes caking) in this area?

Any of these signs can signal an illness, and although some of them may be easy to correct, others may be difficult. These signs (or symptoms), their causes, and their treatments are discussed in this book, arranged alphabetically in order to give you quick and easy access.

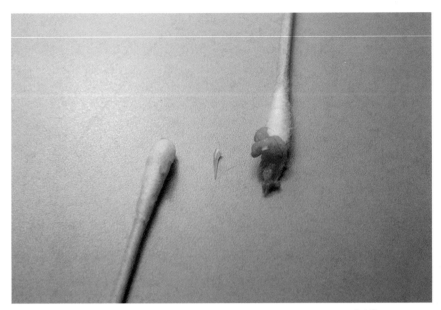

▲ A Burmese python was presented with membrane protruding above the lower lip, a sign of mouth rot. This photo shows the caseated pus and dead tissue removed from the lip, and also an infected tooth that was removed and apparently was the source of the infection. Photo by Roger Klingenberg, D.V.M.

Treating a Snake

First, because most snakes do not vocalize or have obvious facial expressions that indicate pain, many herpetoculturists have been tempted to treat their own snakes, up to and including minor surgeries (sometimes without anesthesia)! Make no mistake, snakes *do* feel pain. Anyone who has given an injection of an antibiotic to a ball python *(Python regius)* has seen it jump. Keep this in mind as you consider the home treatment of your pet.

Secondly, most reptile-oriented veterinarians believe that oral antibiotics are useless in the treatment of *most* infectious diseases of snakes. Thus, the purchase of over-the-counter oral antibiotics is not only a waste of your money but also a waste of valuable time. During this time, the disease may progress beyond a point at which it can be treated, even with professional help. Remember this as you consider home treatment.

Lastly, the anatomy and physiology of snakes are different from that of many other animals. There are even marked differences among snakes. For one thing, snakes have a renal portal system, which means basically that all the blood in the back half of the body is filtered through the kidneys before circulating to the front of the body. In other words, any antibiotics that are to be injected should be injected in the *front* half of the body. Most antibiotics also should be injected intramuscularly (in the muscle). If you have never administered an injection to a snake or seen it done by a professional, you may be wasting your time, and you could injure the snake. Consider this possibility before you attempt home treatment. Bear in mind also that the choice of antibiotics is not an arbitrary one. Different antibiotics have different characteristics and are effective against different bacteria. In most cases, the choice should be based upon a culture and a sensitivity test. It is important to note, however, that an educated guess on the correct antibiotic must be made prior to the return of the results of the culture and sensitivity test, and it should be administered immediately. This is a situation in which experience really counts. The antibiotic chosen can always be changed if the results show that the educated guess is incorrect.

Finally, the proper dose must be administered. The proper drug administered at the wrong dose is actually a poison that may cause organ damage or death. Even the proper doses administered improperly are potentially dangerous or, at best, useless. A highly irritating substance accidentally injected into the lung may cause a tremendous local reaction leading to pneumonia. The injection of the same antibiotic subcutaneously (under the skin) will not be absorbed and distributed properly, thereby negating much of its effectiveness.

Thus, there are several things that need to be taken into consideration prior to attempting the treatment of your own snake(s). Many veterinarians can now provide a great deal of assistance in diagnosing and treating snakes.

Although there are many things (discussed in detail in this book) that you can do to help your snakes, their *best* chance for survival is to have the attention of an experienced reptile veterinarian.

Abscesses

The most common cause of lumps or bumps in reptiles is an abscess: a pocket of bacteria and dead cells. The bacteria that form abscesses may invade the area locally from the skin or through the blood (hematogenously). The presence of an abscess strongly suggests that the reptile

▲ *Anal gland abscessing in a hognose snake.*

has been housed in such a manner that its immune system is not functioning properly. Therefore, the animal's housing conditions need to be corrected as part of the treatment.

If you have a strong stomach, you can treat superficial abscesses at home by slicing them open and flushing them with a povidone iodine solution. Reptile pus is usually solid, not liquid, so you need to make sure that you remove the pus manually; don't expect it to drain by itself. You may do so by applying pressure to the sides of the abscess and then using *curettage* (scraping out the inside of the abscess with a small spoon-like instrument) after you have expressed the majority of the pus through the incision you have made. Then, as there is a reason those abscesses formed, check the snake's environment: Is it warm enough, dry enough, clean enough? The presence of one abscess that you do see may be a warning that there are other abscesses you do not see. Accordingly, the treatment of abscesses almost always requires the use of systemic antibiotics along with removing the abscesses.

You should base the selection of an appropriate antibiotic upon a culture and a sensitivity test of the purulent material itself or of the inner wall of the abscess. If you drain the abscess at home, you must immediately take a sample of the pus (in a manner that precludes contamination from outside organisms) to your reptile veterinarian.

If you slice open a lump and find a parasite, wash your hands immediately, and take your snake to a reptile-oriented veterinarian at once. This is probably sparganosis (a tapeworm imbedded in the muscle or just under the skin), and it is a more serious problem than the average snake keeper can handle, because the worms are usually distributed throughout the snake, not just in one lump.

Anorexia and Inappetance
(Not Eating)

Inappetance is the second-most frustrating problem (after sudden death) that we deal with as herpetoculturists and veterinarians. There are a number of reasons for its occurrence and a number of solutions. We have grouped these reasons for purposes of our discussion, but several factors may be at play in any one case of anorexia.

Environmental Factors

Perhaps the most common reasons for failure to feed are environmental. Temperature and/or humidity increases or decreases, which may be imperceptible to the owner, may trigger a loss of appetite in a captive snake, even a long-term captive. Maintaining a snake in a cage with a thermal gradient that approaches its preferred optimum temperature range (POTR) for day and night cycles help its appetite.

Shortening of the photophase in the fall or winter also may be responsible for the sudden onset of inappetance. If there is a window in the room where the snake is maintained, inappetance may occur even if artificial lighting is provided. Some species cue in on the natural light cycles, regardless of the artificial light cycle you may offer. At the opposite extreme, excessive lighting—continuous light—can result in anorexia. And the quality and intensity of the light you provide may contribute to a loss of appetite if that light is not appropriate for a particular species or an individual specimen.

Seasonal barometric pressure variations have been shown to be important in the activity patterns of some amphibians and reptiles, and presumably these may affect their appetite as well. Remember: Anorexia is a normal, self-protective mechanism for many temperate-zone reptiles in preparation for hibernation (brumation). Force-feeding during this time is usually uncalled for and may result in trauma, leading to anorexia later.

The substrate (cage bottom material) is often found to be a cause in cases of anorexia. Certainly, secretive snakes like the Arizona coral snake *(Micruroides euryxanthus)* or a shovelnose snake genus *Chionactis* may refuse to feed unless they are provided with a good burrowing medium such as mulch or sand. Similarly, arboreal snakes may refuse to feed if they are not provided with stable branches. Cage size is another extremely important captive environmental factor. Many a snake will begin feeding after it is placed in a larger or smaller cage, depending upon its needs. Of course, you should research all of these factors before the arrival of the animal in question.

Dietary Preference Factors

The dietary preferences of certain animals are well known. Unfortunately, the preferred diets of many species are either unknown or not readily available to the herpetoculturist. Substitution may or may not be acceptable to the snake in question, and even "clean" mice and rats may not consitute a balanced diet for some species.

Examples of substitutes that are unacceptable to the palates of some captive snakes include waxworms instead of ants for some blind snakes *(Leptotyphlops),* and domestic mice instead of lizards for some gray-banded kingsnakes *(Lampropeltis alterna).* Many herpetoculturists have become extremely ingenious at tricking their carnivorous snakes into feeding by utilizing scent-transfer techniques: rubbing a preferred food item on a readily available domestic item. Some individuals will take only dead food, while others will accept only live food. Some will take dead prey, but only when you shake it in their face while holding

▲ Overcrowding snakes causes a psychological and disease-originating nightmare. The crowded animals typically refuse to eat, are stressed by constant disturbance (resulting in suppression of their immune systems) while they are exposed to a wide variety of disease-causing bacteria and parasites from other snakes, some of which may be from different continents.

it in long tongs or forceps. The *size* of the prey item offered also can be relevant to many different serpents such as sharptail snakes *(Contia tenuis)* and rock rattle-snakes *(Crotalus lepidus)*. Some snakes will settle only for the "real thing" and if not provided with it will starve to death. Fortunately, these cases are the minority. [See the section on *Feeding*.]

Psychological Factors

Psychological factors have only recently received a great deal of attention from herpetoculturists. The location of a cage, its stability, and visibility of the surroundings may negatively affect a snake's appetite. The presence of more than one snake in the same cage may inhibit the feeding of a submissive one, and of every snake present if they are all nervous or territorial animals. Frequent handling by the keeper, frequent passersbys, and even frequent cleaning also may inhibit feeding. Prey sometimes may injure an otherwise good feeder, which as a result becomes "mouse shy." Therefore, it is always advisable to house snakes singly, in stable cages, with restricted visibility. Handle a

▲ *Baby snake impacted with corn cob bedding.* Photo by Don Swerida, D.V.M.

snake less frequently if it is a finicky eater and, in most cases (except for insectivores), offer it pre-killed prey whenever possible.

Of course, periods of anorexia are natural for many snakes, particularly just prior to shedding and during the hibernation or winter rest period. Male snakes during breeding season and gestating female snakes also stop feeding as a matter of course.

Overfeeding a snake may cause fasting later on but is not a cause for concern. Some specimens binge and then fast as part of their normal eating habits, a process that may be tied to natural cycles of food availability in the wild.

Medical Factors

Medical reasons for anorexia in reptiles are numerous. Perhaps the most common reason is parasites, especially if the reptiles have been captured recently. Long-term captives also are vulnerable if they either have never been treated or have not been treated recently. We strongly advise regular fecal exams and treatments. Intestinal impactions caused by the ingestion of improper substrates,

▲ *Proper enclosure size and cleanliness is essential for the good health and longevity of your snake.*

such as small-size gravel or ground corncob, are a close second cause of anorexia in smaller snakes. Infections involving any or all systems—including respiratory, intestinal, or integumentary—are other common reasons for inappetence. We can certainly understand how a snake with a bad case of stomatitis (mouth rot) or pneumonia may not have the desire to feed, but any infection also is capable of causing anorexia. Metabolic problems caused by excesses or deficiencies of various minerals, vitamins, or hormones also may cause appetite loss; one example is hyperthyroidism in older rat snakes genus *Elaphe*. Nor are snakes immune to health problems such as diabetes or kidney failure. Tumors, trauma, and toxins can all cause anorexia as well. Sensory loss, especially loss of the extremely important senses of smell and sight, may account for an inexplicable failure to feed; check for an intact tongue in a recently captured snake that only shows interest in live, moving prey, never pre-killed. Incidentally, sight does not seem as important as smell in the feeding response of many snakes. Yet the feeding patterns of diurnal snakes with large eyes, which are very visually oriented, may be expected to be negatively affected by the loss of one or both eyes through trauma or infection.

One of the more pleasant medical reasons for anorexia in female snakes is that they are gravid. As the embryos develop, they apparently occupy a good deal of space in the animal's body, and some believe this condition inhibits feeding. Pregnancy is not so pleasant, however, if an anorexic gravid female is very malnourished, has a severe infection that has spread to the uterus, or has some other life-threatening difficulty that may lead to dystocia (egg binding), yolk emboli, yolk peritonitis, uterine rupture, retained products of conception, infertility, or death.

Maladaptation

Maladaptation Syndrome (Cowan, 1980) may be defined as pathological effects in an animal associated with the stress of captivity. One example of this syndrome is the deterioration of the pancreas in a number of species of rattlesnakes genus *Crotalus* when they first arrive in captivity. Prior to and aside from medical problems, however, come the sickening behavioral signs: constant

▼Natural caging with hot spots and numerous hiding places may be required for some "difficult" snakes. Most of the more commonly kept snakes do well in a much simpler environment, however.

movement within the cage, abrasion of the nose, failure to feed, and eventually, cachexia (wasting away), followed by disease and death.

It is important to note that the majority of medical and psychological problems, perhaps 90 percent, are either directly or indirectly related to environmental problems. Maladaptation syndrome may be avoided in some cases by creating an environment very similar to that from which the animal was derived. It is critical to examine and reexamine thoroughly the environment of every anorexic snake and to make the best possible corrections. There are no medical miracles that will save these animals if their environments are not improved first. Force-feeding is only palliative in most cases, and it is usually unnecessary *if* the environment has first been corrected. Multivitamin injections or metronidazole at a dose of 40 milligrams per kilogram orally will sometimes stimulate a snake to begin eating.

Burns

Sadly, thermal burns are among the most common problems of captive snakes. In many cases, these injuries can be avoided if you exercise common sense and regularly observe the snakes in your care. Although treatment is possible, it is often a prolonged, expensive, and painful experience, both for the owner and for the snake, with permanent scarring a typical outcome. The major goal of this section is to help prevent burns from occurring, although we discuss the treatment here as well. [See also the section on *Dermatitis*.]

Burns can usually be prevented by following several simple rules.

1. Do not place any heating device (heating pads, heat tapes, and even lights) inside the cage or anywhere that the snake can come in direct contact with it. Because "hot rocks" are incriminated in many burn cases, we do not recommend them. Do *not* assume that the snake will avoid contact with something that is very hot. Following this rule will also prevent your snake from accidentally electrocuting itself if it spills its water bowl.

2. Do not heat the entire floor or top of a cage. Heating only a portion of the enclosure will allow the snake to thermoregulate and to select cool areas according to its needs.

▲ *Digital indoor/ outdoor thermometer. These inexpensive thermometers can be used to monitor temperatures accurately during hibernation or transportation. Keeping accurate temperature records is often tremendously helpful in making management decisions.*

3. Do not place the snake's cage in direct sunlight, especially if it is a glass cage.

4. Make sure that the cage is well ventilated; doing this will allow excess heat to rise and escape the enclosure, thereby affording the snake extra protection from over-heating.

5. Buy and use a thermometer.

6. Check your heating devices regularly by feeling the heated areas.

Treatment of burns is much more difficult than their prevention. The first step in treating any burn is to remove its source; however, this must be done without removing the snake's heat source altogether. To do so will compromise the snake's immune response just when it may be needed most. Use a good gentle heat source as part of the treatment regime. Afterward, you should apply topical antibiotics such as Polysporin® ointment, Silvadene Cream 1%® (Marion Labs), or a povidone iodine ointment such as Betadine® to the lesions each day for a period of a few weeks to one month. In many cases, it is advisable to allow the snake to soak in a povidine iodine solution for 30 minutes per day prior to applying the ointment.

In severe cases, which most burns are, injectable antibiotics are necessary and will help the snake recover. [See the section on *Dermatitis* (skin lesions) and the section on *Medicines*.] Your reptile veterinarian will probably recommend that the skin lesions be cultured, in order to determine which antibiotic is the best one to use. Depending upon the severity of the burn, it may require two to four weeks of an injectable antibiotic and four to eight weeks of one of the topical medications previously mentioned.

Burns heal slowly. Extensive burns commonly require numerous ecdyses (skin sheddings) in order to heal. These burned areas may slough the epidermal layer completely, exposing raw, seeping tissue underneath. With each shedding, however, these areas will grow smaller and smaller, until they are completely healed. Scarring is the norm, rather than the exception, with burned snakes, leaving a permanent reminder of the incident. [See the section on *Dermatitis* (skin lesions) for more information.]

Remember: Burns are serious and possibly fatal events that are *much* more easily prevented than cured.

Constipation

Overfed, underactive snakes are prime candidates for constipation. Other factors that can contribute to constipation are slightly cooler temperatures than usual and slightly lower humidity. Cooler air temperatures can cause a snake to "hug" its heat source, and by doing so, the inactive snake essentially "cooks" the stool in its colon for several days, thereby drying it out and making it more difficult to pass. Lower cage humidity increases the rate of evaporative water loss even more and worsens an already serious situation. Without any intervention, the snake's stools may became as hard and dry as rocks, which is why they are called *fecoliths*, meaning "fecal stones." Chronic constipation or obstipation may result in quite a backup, especially as many snakes continue eating during this time.

There are a number of treatments for constipation or obstipation. The first and most important is to correct the environment. Eliminate drying substates such as corn-cob litter, and remove wood and cardboard fixtures from the cage. Avoid using cages with sides made of untreated wood, as these may also dry out the air within the cage. Finally, consider using a humidifier near the cage. Increasing your snake's exercise by increasing the size of the cage

▲ Dry air, small
cages, and lack of
exercise, as well as
an excessively
warm ventral heat
source, may all
contribute to a
snake's
constipation. Warm-
water soaks and
laxatives may be
helpful, but if not,
don't wait long
before seeking
veterinary attention.
Photo by Steve Barten,
D.V.M.

and cage accessories, reducing the frequency of feeding,
and feeding it smaller, more digestible items, may also
help to alleviate this problem.

The next step in treating constipation is to try several
warm water soaks. Usually, placing the snake in shallow
warm water fifteen minutes per day for three or four days
will cause it to defecate. If not, an enema of warm water or
of a very dilute solution of dioctyl sodium sulfosuccinate
(DSS) will likely work. Frye (1991) quotes Paul-Murphy
and others (1987) in advising that DSS be diluted at a ratio
of one part DSS (standard stock solution) to 20 parts water
if the solution is to be administered through a stomach
tube. Frye also advises the use of magnesium oxide (Milk
of Magnesia®) suspension or mineral oil in small amounts
as aids for constipation.

A small quantity of mineral oil (one milliliter per
kilogram of body weight) administered through a stomach
tube has long been recommended and, indeed, does seem
to work. The administration must be made by one experi-

enced in tubing reptiles, however, as the improper placement may lead to regurgitation as well as aspiration of the oil, with resultant pneumonia. One means of administering the mineral oil that we have found successful over the years has been jokingly referred to by the senior author as "mouse lax" or "rat lax." Basically, if a snake is still feeding, you can offer a pre-killed mouse or rat that has been injected with the appropriate dose of mineral oil (hence the name). Several days later, when the mouse or rat is digested, the oil is released, the stool is softened, and defecation occurs within several days to a few weeks. Some sources have suggested that calcium supplementation by injection could be useful in treating this problem because it would improve muscle tone, but we have not yet tested this method.

If the medical approach is unsuccessful, surgical removal of the fecoliths is necessary. Generally speaking, however, the best approach to this problem is prevention. Avoid overfeeding your snake, provide it with as much room as possible, and maintain appropriate temperature and humidity ranges. Although some sources have suggested that routine handling may be good exercise for the snake, remember that some animals do not tolerate handling very well.

Dehydration

Like other animals, snakes may become dehydrated. In most cases, the causes are lack of drinking water and consistently high temperatures inside the cage. Some caging materials and substrates will also contribute to this problem. Bare, untreated wood cages are notoriously hygroscopic (absorbent of air humidity), as well as abrasive and difficult to disinfect. Substrates such as corn-cob litter are also hygroscopic. We therefore advise the keeper to avoid wooden cages, drying substrates, and excessive heat. You also should regularly provide water for most snakes, and at all times for others. House your snakes in smooth-sided enclosures constructed of nonporous materials such as glass, plastic, metal, or melamine-coated wood. Research the available literature for the specific substrates that have worked well for previous keepers of your species.

If a snake, particularly a small one, appears seriously dehydrated (its skin has wrinkles that return very slowly or not at all to their original position when gently pulled away from the body), you should get the snake to a veterinarian right away. It may need emergency fluids or tube feeding. If you cannot reach a veterinarian immediately, you may administer an electrolyte solution such as dilute Pedialyte® (mix it with an equal quantity of water to produce a half-strength solution) through a stomach tube (about two to three milliliters per 100 grams of body

▲ *This ball python has definite signs of dehydration.*

weight per day for several days, or until seen by a veterinarian). A new product named Reptilaid®, which is specifically formulated for dehydrated reptiles, is an excellent alternative. A veterinarian will administer about 20 milliliters of a sterile electrolyte solution per kilogram of body weight intraperitoneally once per day for several days. Note: an injection in the abdominal cavity must be done with caution to avoid abdominal structures and *only* in the caudal (back) one-third of the body to avoid the lungs. The most frequent solution used is lactated Ringer's, although Jarchow's solution (two parts 2.5 percent dextrose in 0.45 percent salt plus one part Ringer's) is theoretically a better alternative (Jarchow 1988). Extremely dehydrated snakes may benefit from an intracardiac catheter as perfected by Mader (1992).

Keep the snake warm, but remember that increased temperatures will increase the rate of dehydration. Remember: It is sometimes difficult to differentiate between a very thin snake (i.e., one suffering from starvation) and a dehydrated snake. Anorexia (failure to eat) and problems complicated by weight loss are discussed elsewhere in this book.

Dermatitis (Skin Lesions)

Burns, bite wounds, abrasions, retained skin from an
attempted shed, skin tumors, parasites, excessive moisture
of the substrate or high humidity, and filthy cages may all
predispose snakes to dermatitis (an infection of the skin),
by allowing the entry of bacteria. Most skin lesions in
snakes are occupied by bacteria, rather than caused by
them. Veterinarians regard this kind of infection as a
secondary infection and look for causes among those listed
above. Once the bacteria become established, they become
a major factor in the course of the disease and must be
treated in order to save the infected animal. Without
antibiotics in the bloodstream (usually administered to
reptiles by injection), bacteria may spread rapidly, causing
abscesses, stomatitis (infection in the mouth), pneumonia,
cellulitis (infection into deeper tissues, causing a swollen
appearance of an area), septicemia (bacteria in the bloodstream), and death. As we have previously pointed out,
the antibiotics chosen should be based upon a culture and
sensitivity test, and ideally, the primary cause should be
determined (by biopsy, if necessary) and eliminated.

Dermatitis may be caused by fungi, worms, or possibly even a viral invader. (A virus has not yet been isolated
from skin lesions in snakes, although one has been in
lizards.) Worms and mites may be treated with the
appropriate antiparasitic agent, which is discussed later in

▲ Spontaneous skin splitting. This lesion usually occurs in young snakes and is presently thought to be due to malnourishment. Immediate surgery may reduce the scarring, but the cause of the nutritional problem must be determined and eliminated if possible.

this book. Suspected tumors need to be surgically removed. Retained shed skin or other factors contributing to the dermatitis should be eliminated. Fungal lesions and fungal infections will respond to warmth, dryness, and daily applications of povidone iodine, such as Betadine® or in combination with one of many antifungal ointments, including Tinactin®, Micatin®, and Veltrim®. We have also had limited success with a diluted extract of melaleuca, and this may be worth looking into more thoroughly. So far, we have not found systemic antifungal agents used in mammals and other reptiles to work well in snakes, although both Nystatin and Pulvicin have been tried.

Fungal and bacterial infections alike may take more than a month of daily applications in order to heal. We generally place the snake in a container into which we have placed paper towels soaked in dilute Betadine® solution and we leave the animal there for 30 to 60 minutes. We then remove the snake, rinse it off, and apply the antifungal ointment to its lesions.

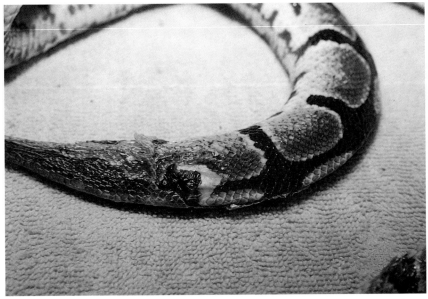

▲ *Tearing of the skin of a malnourished ball python. Chronic starvation often results in thin skin, which tears easily.*

Infections that are primarily bacterial have responded nicely to the Betadine® bath treatment alone, or to the bath followed by one of a number of antibacterial topicals. Sometimes these topicals work well even when used alone. Silvadine Cream® one percent is an excellent topical for reptiles (Rosskopf, 1992); it has become very popular recently. Polysporin® ointment also works well. As with any infection in snakes, supplemental heat is a good idea, but remember that it will increase evaporation, so the snake must have access to water at *all* times. Also, remember that the use of artificial turf is therapeutic for many skin lesions because it allows fresh air to circulate under the snake. We have seen many minor lesions heal without any antibiotics when snakes have been housed on clean, dry artificial turf.

If you can see no response to environmental correction and topical medications, consult a veterinarian to diagnose the specific cause of the skin lesions. The veterinarian may

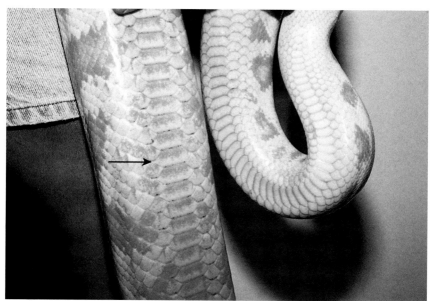

▲ A change in the texture and color of the skin often signifies a bacterial or fungal infection, as seen in this albino Burmese python. Note the small dark spots between the scales. This turned out to be a fungal infection.

choose to perform a biopsy and culture and sensitivity tests in order to determine the best way to cure the skin problem, and to determine which antibiotic is best for the infection. [See Jacobson (1992) or Rossi (1996) for a more detailed discussion on reptile dermatology.]

Diarrhea

Diarrhea is the occurrence of loose, watery, and usually foul-smelling stools. The causes of diarrhea in snakes are similar to those that cause vomiting, and in many cases both symptoms occur. As with vomiting (and indeed with most other medical problems in snakes), the first part of the treatment for diarrhea is to correct the environment. If the problem persists, then you must seek a medical solution. Repeated fecal exams or a gastric wash may reveal protozoan or metazoan parasites, and a fecal culture and sensitivity test may reveal primary or secondary bacterial invaders causing the loose stools. Once the nature of the guilty organism is determined, it may be eliminated with an appropriate parasiticide or antibiotic.

A veterinarian may also replace fluid losses and provide supportive care. Sometimes diarrhea will respond to increased environmental temperature alone. But do not delay treatment long, or it may become a very serious, if not fatal, problem. Frye (1991) advises the use of Kaopectate® at a dose directly related to the weight of the snake. We have used a dose of one milliliter per kilogram of body weight successfully on small snakes. Do not handle the snake at all until after the diarrhea stops except as is necessary to treat the animal. [See the section on *Dehydration* for further suggestions.

▲ Normal snake stool is dark brown or black and usually fairly solid. The white portion is uric acid, the normal product of the urinary tract in snakes. Any discoloration should concern the keeper.

Remember that loose, foul-smelling stools may be normal for any snake being fed a diet that is primarily fish or amphibian. Less odorous and firmer stools may form immediately after switching that snake's diet to scented mice.

Dysecdysis (Improper Shedding)

Most captive snakes shed every one to three months,
preceded by a "blueing" of the skin and eyes, which then
partially return to normal just prior to the actual shed.
Healthy snakes, maintained properly, will usually shed
their skin in one piece. Normal shedding is called ecdysis.
Difficult shedding in many pieces is referred to as
dysecdysis and may be caused by parasites, malnutrition,
infection, metabolic irregularities, tumors, or (*usually*),
poor environment: the relative humidity is too low, the
substrate is too drying, there is no slightly rough surface to
rub against, and so on. In other words, most shedding
problems may be avoided by correcting the environment.

If a snake needs help immediately, place it in a warm,
wet pillowcase for 30 minutes to an hour. Don't forget to
tie the top! Do not place the pillowcase anywhere that
water could overflow and cover the bag! And do not place
the pillowcase where the snake can fall or get stepped on!
After the prescribed time, you can remove the snake and
usually, if the snake is truly ready to shed, assist with
shedding all of its old skin including the eye shields, or
spectacles. You should remove the spectacles with a wet
cotton-tipped applicator *only* if they don't come off with
the skin. Apply a gentle circular motion for about fifteen
minutes. If you don't succeed during this time, quit and
repeat the whole process again in a few days, or quit and

Most shedding
problems may be
avoided by
correcting the
environment

▲ Dysecdysis (improper shedding) commonly occurs when environments are too drying. It is particularly seen in the winter, when homes are artificially heated. Wooden cages and drying substrates, such as corncob litter, may also contribute to the problem, as can mites. Photo by Steve Barten, D.V.M.

see a reptile-oriented veterinarian. If you force a spectacle off before it is ready, you could expose the cornea, and the snake could lose the eye.

Some of the products sold over the counter to help snakes shed are no more than expensive soap mixtures. That is not to say that they do not help; they do, by helping water enter the old skin. But you can achieve the same effect by using a small amount of mild dishwashing detergent such as Ivory® or Dove® in the soaking process described above. A dilute solution of one part hydrogen peroxide to three or four parts water has also been found to help snakes shed more easily.

Egg Care

Although we do not intend this book to be a breeding manual, the deposition of eggs may immediately thrust the snake keeper into a critical situation that requires immediate attention. We provide the following information to assist in the proper delivery of eggs and their care, once they are discovered. This is a cursory discussion of egg care and not intended as a review of all incubation techniques and problems. Refer to any of the excellent references and magazine articles available for more specific information on the care of the eggs of a particular snake species.

Nesting Site

Most female snakes will require a suitable nesting site. Otherwise, they will refuse to lay their eggs or will lay them in inappropriate places, like their water bowl! For most snakes, a nesting site will consist of a secluded area with a semimoist medium. Sphagnum moss or vermiculite, lightly mixed with water, have been used as egg-laying media with excellent success. For most snakes, plastic shoe or sweater boxes make ideal egg-laying boxes. Simply cut a small hole in one side—or preferably the top—of the box. Top holes are preferable because with side holes, many snakes will push much of the medium out of the box in an effort to find the best spot in which to lay their eggs. Also, remember to secure the top well or

▲ *Hatchling Baird's rat snakes, a popular captive-bred species. Separate these babies as soon as possible to avoid undue stress.*

the snake may pop it off. Some people have used the large plastic dog carriers or cat carriers for larger snakes such as pythons.

Place the egg-laying box in the cage several days to a few weeks prior to expected egg laying, in order to allow the female to learn of its presence and become comfortable with it. Many snakes have what has been termed a pre-laying shed within two to four weeks of egg laying. Look for this shed and be prepared for imminent egg laying.

Once the eggs are deposited, move them to an incubation box. (Some python keepers choose to leave the eggs with the mother for incubation, but this is risky unless the temperature and humidity of the cage are reasonably close to proper levels.) Incubation boxes are commonly airtight containers in which the snake keeper has placed a vermiculite and water mixture. The ratio of the mixture has been the topic of a great deal of discussion recently, but we find that a ratio of less than one part water to one part vermiculite (by weight) is suitable. Some authorities have suggested that a ratio of one-half part water to one part vermiculite (by weight) is safer and more likely to result in bigger, healthier babies (Hammack, 1991). Many other substrates have been used and these are discussed in detail in many other references. The incubation period generally ranges from 30 to 90 days for most snakes, depending upon the species. Suitable incubation temperatures for pythons range from 88 to 91° F (31 to 33° C), while suitable incubation temperatures for most colubrids may fluctuate from 70 to 88° F (21 to 31° C). You must remember to open the incubator frequently (five minutes every two to three days) during incubation to allow some air to enter the incubation box. Oxygen requirements are believed to increase as the embryos develop; therefore, you should probably increase the frequency of opening towards the latter part of the incubation period. Indeed, some herpetoculturists have proposed that failure to do so is likely responsible for late-term death of an embryo in the egg. Also, be certain not to cause excess vibration or rotation of the eggs.

If the eggs begin to cave in, they may be in an incubating medium that is too dry, so make sure that they are set up as we have described. Another all too common and frustrating reason for an egg to cave in, is that it is infertile. If "weeping" of the eggs occurs in early incubation, it usually means that the eggs were laid prematurely, and they are most likely to die. If mold begins to grow as the eggs cave in, the eggs were probably infertile to begin with; however, many healthy little snakes have hatched out of eggs that have been covered with mold. Generally speaking, if the egg retains its shape, the young snake is probably still alive. We usually recommend giving all eggs the benefit of the doubt and not disturbing them until after the other eggs in the clutch have started to hatch.

Late-term death of fully developed embryos is a frustrating and common occurrence in snake egg incubation at the time of this writing. Presently, it is believed that this may be caused by an oxygen deficiency as previously discussed.

Normal hatching usually takes several days as the snakes pip (slice through their eggs) and remain in the egg while they convert from egg-membrane respiration to pulmonary respiration. Thus, you must *not* remove the young snakes from these eggs prematurely. If most of the eggs have hatched and one or two healthy appearing ones remain unpipped, you may decide to intervene. Carefully slice the top of the egg to create a small window, and peer into the egg. You can do this with a pair of surgical forceps and a scalpel. Grasp the top of the shell with forceps and gently pull upward. Then gently slice the "tented" area with the scalpel. Carefully extend the incision and then extend it at a right angle from the initial incision. It has been our experience that the embryo is likely to be alive if clear albumen is rapidly expelled from the egg. Milky-appearing albumen or thickened albumen that is not rapidly expelled are usually indicative of a dead embryo. If you observe a live snake, leave it alone and allow it several more days to emerge from that egg; some individuals take longer than others. When the snake does emerge, check it for an egg tooth. Some herpetoculturists have suggested that many of these non-hatching live snakes are lacking an egg tooth. If this is true, and it turns out to be a genetic deficiency, saving the snake and breeding it may introduce a tremendously harmful gene into the captive snake population. As yet, however, the cause of this defect is undetermined for certain.

Note: Hatchling snakes in their eggs may attract carrion flies. These flies may lay their eggs inside snake eggs that have pipped but have not yet hatched, thereby threatening the young snakes. For this reason, we usually keep the top on our egg-laying boxes right though hatching, even though we remove and replace it frequently in the process of checking on the hatchlings.

You should house hatchling snakes in a manner similar to that of adults, keeping in mind that access to a high-humidity area is especially important for them. This high-humidity area can be a plastic box stuffed with semimoist sphagnum moss. They are called humidity boxes, but actually they are the same as the egg-laying boxes previously described. These hatchlings, like the newborn of live-bearing snakes, will usually shed within a few days to a few weeks, and they may refuse food until after their first shed. [See the discussion on *Perinatology*.]

Escape (Management of)

Properly housed snakes will never escape from their cages; however, nothing in the world is perfect, and occasionally one will get away. Following is some advice on how to get it back. (This information can also be used as advice for "normal" snake-fearing people to round up an unwanted visitor from their homes without harming the snake.)

When looking for a lost snake, the best time is at night, at least 30 minutes after all lights in the house are turned off. Funneled minnow traps, glue boards, and piles of towels are the best trapping devices, placed where the snake was last seen. Usually, this area is in some corner or along a wall of the room in which the snake was maintained.

Minnow traps can and will trap many small snakes, and you can pick up even small venomous snakes with a garden tool or a thick blanket after they have become trapped in these little enclosures. Once the snake is back in its cage or outside, the traps can be opened easily.

Glue boards, like those used for mice and rats, can also be placed in areas traveled by escaped or visiting snakes. You can nail the glue board to a long board so that even venomous snakes can be picked up safely after they have become stuck. Then you can pour vegetable oil on the glue board to release the snake after it is back in its cage or outside.

▲ Fractured neck. This snake escaped and got its head stuck under a door. For health reasons, and in keeping with American Federation of Herpetoculturists (A.F.H.) policies, snakes should be securely caged.

A pile of old towels or burlap bags is an old and very successful method for capture. Give the pile several days in the proper location, then go through it to see if your missing snake has entered it. Of course, if you are advising this trick to someone who does not like snakes and is unaware whether they are dealing with a venomous snake or not, have them pick up the whole pile of towels with a shovel and carry it outside, where they can safely examine the pile with the shovel. If the snake is uncovered, it will usually flee at once, never to be seen again.

Finally, there is the live-bait trap. You can place a live mouse or rat in a bird cage or an aquarium that has a secure screen top with a small hole in its center. The snake may enter the cage or aquarium, eat the rodent, and be trapped until the meal is digested. The crucial element here is the size of the hole. It must be just large enough that a snake can pass through it with an empty stomach, but *not* with a prey bulge.

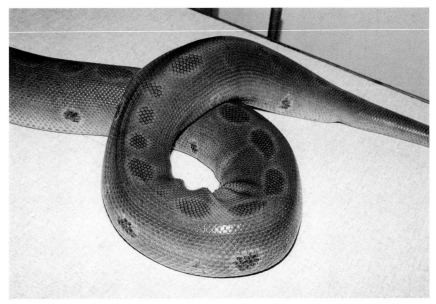

▲ *Paralyzed green Burmese python. This snake escaped and injured it's back. This a another reason why large constrictors should be confined.*

In Ecuador, they capture snakes by tying a dead rodent to a stake. The snake swallows the rodent, cord and all, and is trapped by becoming affixed to the stake.

One last trick is worth mentioning. If an escape occurs during cool weather, consider turning up the heat in the house. This method has been known to bring many snakes out of hiding.

Remember to check the snake thoroughly after it is recaptured. Abrasions, splinters, and lacerations may require some treatment. Exotic snakes may become chilled during their wanderings and end up with respiratory infections or stomatitis (mouth rot). Antibiotics may be required.

As longtime snake keepers, we are aware of the frustration of the so-called empty-cage syndrome. We hope these tips will aid in your recovery from this stress by helping you capture your little wanderer. And remember, this is great advice you can give to people who fear snakes. It will help them rid their homes of snakes without killing them, thereby benefiting both parties. Good luck!

Be a responsible snake owner and prevent escapes by utilizing appropriate and secure cages and by double checking the lids or door regularly. Also seal all holes and cracks in walls, floors, and such as soon as you become a snake owner, thereby simplifying the recapture of an escapee.

The authors would like to thank Pat Grace, University of Florida Extension Agent, for some of the previously discussed suggestions.

Feeding Frequency
and Obesity

One of the questions most commonly asked of reptile veterinarians is how frequently a snake should be fed. This is an important question and its answer has been arrived at in several ways. Studies of wild snakes have revealed that temperate-zone snakes generally consume two to four times their body weight in food per year (Fitch, 1982). Inactive species and individuals were expected to have requirements closer to the bottom end of this range, while very active snakes were expected to have requirements closer to the upper end. Using this information as a guideline, and considering that most captive snakes get little exercise in captivity, the average one-pound snake would require two pounds of mice per year. At an average weight of 50 grams (0.11 pounds), it would take approximately 18 mice per year to maintain a one-pound snake. Assuming an eight-month period of activity and feeding, and four months of hibernation (brumation), this formula translates to one mouse every two weeks to maintain a one-pound snake. Remember that this calculated amount is for a sluggish or inactive snake and does not supply the extra energy that reproduction or growth may require.

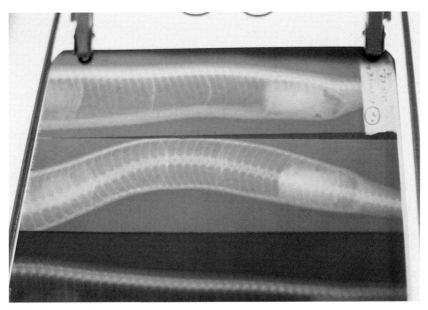

▲ *This is an x-ray of a snake with multiple fecal stones (fecoliths) that required surgical correction.* Photo by Don Swerida, D.V.M.

Using another approach, one can calculate the energy requirement of a snake based upon its metabolic rate. The energy required in Kcals equals ten times the animal's body weight in kilograms to the 0.75 power. Hence, a one-pound snake (0.45 kg) would require 5.5 Kcal per day. Because a mouse is known to contain about 85 Kcal, one mouse would meet the energy requirements of a one-pound snake for 15 days, or approximately two weeks (Mader, 1993), excluding energy for growth or reproduction.

These two methods are reasonably close to predicting the maintenance needs of a one-pound snake, but these levels are far exceeded by most snake keepers, especially snake breeders, who understandably are trying to supply a great deal of excess energy for growth and reproduction. Obesity is commonly the result, especially after the snake's reproduction stops, if the intense feeding regime continues. Males seem to be much more prone to obesity than egg-laying females, thereby supporting the contention of many herpetoculturists that the energy requirements of females may be much higher than those of males.

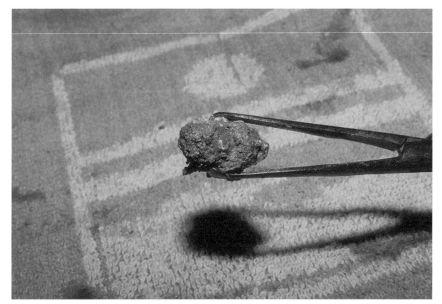

▲ *Surgery was performed and the fecal stone was removed.* Photo by Don Swerida, D.V.M.

This belief is also supported by our observations, and by those of many others, that females of many species are less difficult to please than males of the same species. Perhaps their greater energy demands require that they feed more consistently and with less obvious prey preference than males. [Sexual differences of snakes are discussed in detail in Seigel and Collins, 1993.]

How can you tell if a snake is obese? The two most common signs of obesity are: (1) exposed skin between the scales and (2) inability to coil properly. Another sign of obesity that we have observed is the presence of "fat lines." These are vertical folds in the scales created when a very heavy snake remains coiled for long periods of time. The excess fat creates folds much like "love handles" or "inner tubes" of people, and the scales in the folds bend backwards and become creased.

As in people and other animals, obesity in snakes has been associated with a number of serious health risks. These include heart disease, tumors, lower fertility, metabolic problems, and musculoskeletal problems.

▲ *Reticulated python was so ravenously hungry, it swallowed its own jaw while eating. It required sedation to extract it from the esophagus and put it back in place.*

Captive longevity is also likely to be reduced in obese animals. Therefore, we strongly advise you to feed your snake no more than is necessary for the function needed. Maintenance levels can be calculated using the formula previously cited, but diets for reproduction or growth may require two to three times that amount. Feeding much more than this will usually cause your snake to become seriously overweight.

If a snake is diagnosed as obese, it may be placed on a weight-loss diet. Gradually reduce the intake of the snake down to maintenance levels. To do so, you will need to calculate the maintenance amount as previously shown, basing your calculation on the optimum weight of the snake, and then reducing slowly toward that amount over several months. For example, if a snake is obese, and the maintenance amount is calculated at one mouse per week, but the snake is presently receiving three mice per week, reduce the amount fed as follows. For the first month, reduce the amount fed by 25 percent (12 mice x .75 = 8 mice). The next month, reduce the amount fed by another 25 percent (8 x .75 = 6 mice). By the third month you can usually approach the maintenance level safely. Weigh the snake as frequently as possible to monitor progress.

Never put an obese snake on a starvation diet, as it could cause a number of gastrointestinal or metabolic problems, even though these are rare.

Geriatrics

As the care of snakes improves, their captive life spans appear to be increasing steadily. Snider and Bowler (1992) listed a number of recorded captive longevities of various amphibians and reptiles. It is interesting to note that some snakes now have surpassed the 40-year mark in captivity. At this time, it appears that the pythons and boas are the snakes that live longest, with one boa constrictor (*Boa constrictor*) living more than 40 years and one ball python (*Python regius*) living 47 years. Other snakes, however—including some rattlesnakes genus *Crotalus*, kingsnakes genus *Lampropeltis,* and rat snakes genus *Elaphe*—have exceeded 30 years in captivity. We still do not know whether these figures represent a bias in how many of each group is maintained or their adaptability to captivity, or are truly a reflection of natural life span. There also seems to be a relationship between size and longevity, as there is for many other groups of animals. In any case, more snakes are surviving longer in captivity, and consequently we think it a good idea to discuss some aspects of their care, as well as problems likely to occur in this older group.

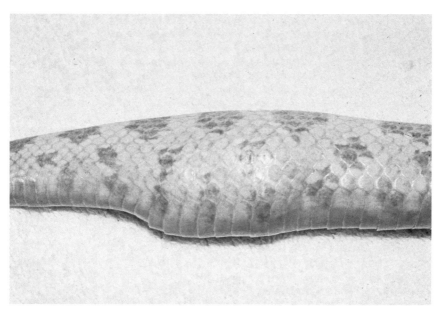

▲ *A renal (kidney) tumor. Old rat snakes (genus* Elaphe) *seem to be especially prone to this problem. If only one kidney is involved, removal of the affected kidney may be possible.*
Photo by Steve Barten, D.V.M.

In general, snakes that have lived to at least 15 years of age have been fairly trim, and none of them has been obese. It is strongly suspected that in snakes, as in mammals, obesity may relate to a number of other health problems, including heart disease and an increased likelihood for tumors, which is why we advise you to avoid excessive feeding of a captive snake. Vertical creases that form in a snake's sides indicate that a snake is becoming obese. If you observe these, a larger cage and smaller, less frequent meals are advisable. Snakes that are bred heavily, long term, may be prime candidates for obesity, once their breeding slows down, particularly if they are sold to a novice snake keeper along with instructions to maintain the same feeding schedule.

Kidney failure has been observed in a number of snakes. It is often associated with overdosing of aminoglycoside antibiotics or chronic dehydration, but changes brought on by aging are a distinct possibility. Water should be available at *all* times for aged snakes, and

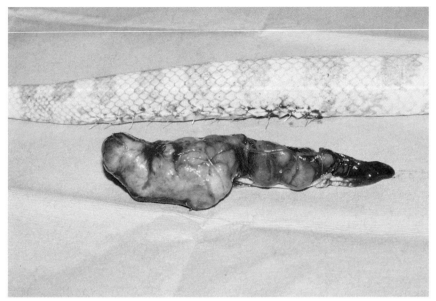

▲ Surgery to remove the tumor was successful.
Photo by Steve Barten, D.V.M.

their cages should never be excessively warm. Large meals and heavy feeding schedules are not required by older, slow-growing senior ophidians. For these snakes, heavy feeding causes extra fat and extra work for their kidneys, which must excrete excess nitrogen.

Cataracts also have been observed in a number of older snakes. Cataracts associated with aging are not life threatening, because good vision is not essential for the feeding response of most captive snakes. Pre-killed food will allow the snake, even an enfeebled one, to make better use of tactile and olfactory cues in securing meals. It is advisable, however, to rule out other causes of cataracts, such as diabetes, by checking with a veterinarian, who will collect blood to determine if there are any metabolic problems. We are just beginning to become aware of the geriatric problems of snakes. In time, much more specific recommendations will be possible. But for now, exercise good judgment and avoid the pitfalls.

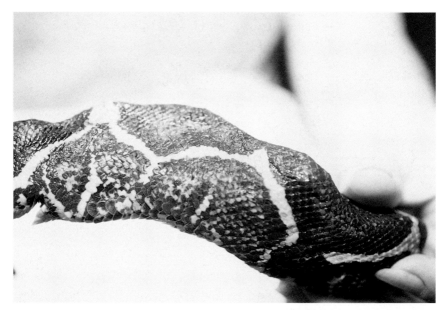

▲ Osteitis deformans in a boa constrictor (Constrictor constrictor). This is a progressive bone disease in which the vertebrae fuse. Its cause is unknown, and there is no treatment. Some experts have suggested that a virus may be responsible. Quarantine your snakes!

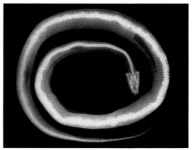

One last interesting point: Neither of us has ever seen an old albino snake. Is this purely a coincidence or is there some connection between albinism and shortened life span in these animals? Funk (1992) suggests that fatty tumors are much more common in albino corn snakes *(Elaphe guttata)* than in other corn snakes. This may be an effect of intensive captive breeding, whereby adults are maintained on a high food-intake regime, or it may be a propensity associated with that particular morph.

Identification

Unfortunately, one of the difficulties of keeping snakes in captivity today is preventing them from being stolen. This task will be much easier if your snake has been marked in such a way that there is no question about its ownership. In the past, keepers have marked snakes by tattooing them or cliping some of their scales. They have also photographed snakes to record distinctive patterns. All of these methods work; however, the latest and best way of identifying snakes is to use an implantable transponder. A number of veterinarians have successfully marked snakes for zoos and private breeders by using these transponders, which are safe and rarely cause any problems. We have used the Destron/IDI Mini-Portable reader and Anicare Microchips (transponders) and have had few problems. The chips, which are no larger than a grain of rice, are injected via a large-gauge needle subcutaneously in most large snakes. In small snakes, the transponder may be carefully injected intraperitoneally, although care must be taken to avoid major organs or blood vessels.

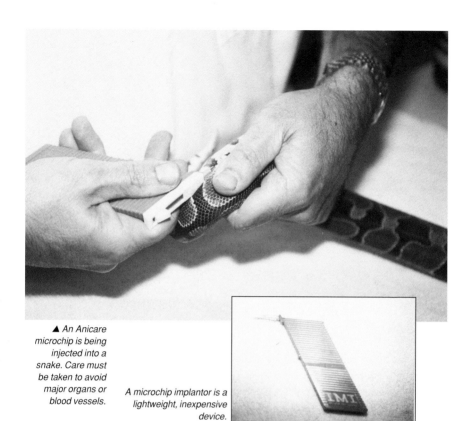

▲ An Anicare microchip is being injected into a snake. Care must be taken to avoid major organs or blood vessels.

A microchip implantor is a lightweight, inexpensive device.

Medicines

Our purpose in writing this book is to acquaint the reader with some of the common maladies of captive snakes, their treatments, and the critical nature of the captive environment. We cannot overemphasize that you should consult an experienced reptile veterinarian before administering antibiotics to a snake. In many cases, amateurs waste valuable time (and money) treating a snake with ineffective drugs or inappropriate doses. This delay may allow an infection to spread, resulting in the death of that animal. Be especially cautious about over-the-counter drugs available in pet shops. Another common outcome is that snakes may suffer kidney damage if they are overdosed.

The following table consists of a number of drugs that a number of veterinarians have found to be effective in treating snakes. Because many snakes are small, and because many amateur keepers may miscalculate their doses, we have added small-snake drug charts. If nothing else, the following charts may help demonstrate how easy it is to overdose or underdose a snake, especially a small one.

These charts can also serve as a quick reference to veterinarians who may be called upon to treat small snakes. The dose recommended in the first column is the dose with which we are most familiar and have used on a

▲ These are four of the most commonly used medicines in snake care today. Metronidazole kills certain protozoans and anaerobic bacteria and stimulates appetite; amikacin is the most commonly used antibiotic; ivermectin is a powerful broad-spectrum deworming agent; and Droncit® kills tapeworms and flukes. Photo by David Campbell.

67

ANTIMICROBIAL SUSCEPTIBILITY REPORT		
	ISOLATE #1	
ANTIMICROBIAL AGENT	MIC	INT
AMIKACIN	**	S
AMPICILLIN	**	R
AUGMENTIN	**	R
CEFOTAXIME	**	I
CEFOXITIN	**	R
CEFTRIAXONE	**	I
CEPHALOTHIN	**	R
CHLORAMPHENICOL	**	R
ENROFLOXACIN	**	S
GENTAMICIN	**	S
NORFLOXACIN	**	S
PIPERACILLIN	**	S
TETRACYCLINE	**	R
TICARCILLIN	**	S
TRIMETH/SULFA	**	R

▲ *A culture and sensitivity tells the veterinarian which antibiotics are likely to be the most effective.*

number of small snakes. These charts also contain doses based upon the metabolic scaling theory, in which the metabolic rate is used to calculate the dose, rather than just the weight of the animal. The doses calculated are based upon reptiles having a K value of 10, compared with K 70 in placental mammals. The K value is a taxonomically dependent constant related to the average body temperature of each group of animals (Sedgewick, et al., 1986, 1988; Mader, 1991). It should be pointed out that it probably varies to some extent between tropical-zone and temperate-zone reptiles, even when they are maintained at the same temperature; however, for the purposes of our discussion, a single K value of 10 was used to calculate these doses. It is quite possible that if one utilizes a lower K value the actual dose may be one-half that listed, and the time between doses may be twice that listed. For very small snakes, virtually no tests have been done to determine the proper dose of many drugs, so this theory is basically a very educated way of guessing the dose. Remember, not all drugs may be calculated this way. The reader is referred to the authors previously cited for a more thorough discussion and techniques of metabolic scaling.

The drugs listed in the following charts are those most commonly used on snakes at the time of this writing. This is not to say that these are the only drugs being administered. For a more thorough discussion of antibiotics useful in all reptiles, consult Frye (1991) and Jacobson (1988). Note that the drug regarded at one time as the "miracle drug" for reptiles is not listed; we have not used Gentocin® injectable for more than five years and can find no benefit to using this drug as compared to the less nephrotoxic and broader spectrum kanamycin derivative, amikacin. We have, however, included a Gentocin® chart comparing the standard recommended dose with the metabolic scaled dose.

Problem / Solution Chart I

Problem	Probable Cause	Solution
Anorexia / Poor Appetite	1.Temperature too low	1. Increase temperature
	2. Prior to shed	2. Wait until shed
	3. Gravid female	3. Wait until eggs are laid
	4. Breeding male	4. Mate or wait
	5. Wrong food offered	5. Offer different food
	6. Overcrowding	6. House Singly
	7. Psychological problem	7. Add hiding places
	8. Mouth infection	8. See veterinarian
	9. Intestinal infection	9. See veterinarian
	10. Respiratory infection	10. See veterinarian
	11. Parasites	11. See veterinarian
	12, Tumor	12. See veterinarian
	13. Too much handling	13. Stop handling
Bumps, Lumps, Blisters, Sores	1. Cage too moist	1. Keep dry; improve ventilation
	2. Cage too dirty	2. Clean cage and disinfect frequently
	3. Parasites	3. See veterinarian or drug chart
	4. Abcesses	4. Slice open and drain or see vet.
	5. Burns	5. Check heat source and see vet.
Constipation	1. Humidity too low	1. Increase humidity
	2. Lack of exercise	2. Increase size of enclosure
	3. Overfeeding	3a. Feed less 3b. Warm water soaks and laxatives
Diarrhea	1. Parasitic or bacterial infection	1. Deworm or see veterinarian
	2. Temperature too low	2. Increase temperature
Dysecdysis / Improper Shed	1. Relative humidity too low	1a. Increase humidity with humidifier 1b. Soak
	2. Water not available or level too low	2. Keep water available and deep enough for soaking when shedding
	3. Mites or ticks	3. Treat parasites
	4. Injuries (old or recent) or infection	4. Assist shedding

Problem / Solution Chart II

Problem	Probable Cause	Solution
Failure to Lay Eggs	1.Not gravid	1. Mate again or wait
	2. Mated later that thought	2. Check records
	3. Egg bound	3. Provide laying box; increase heat and humidity, see veterinarian
	4. Eggs resorbed	4. Feed more, reduce stress, check for parasites, change hibernation tempera- ture, see veterinarian
Open Mouth Breathing, Puffing Throat, Blowing Bubbles, Sneezing	1. Respiratory infection	1. Increase temperature and see vet.
	2. Allergic reaction	2. Change substrate; clean and rinse cage; stop smoking
Stomatitis / Mouth Rot	1. Temperature too low	1. Increase temperature
	2. Trauma	2. Feed dead prey items
	3. Filthy cage	3. Disinfect cage; topical antibiotics; antibiotics; see vet.
Vomiting	1. Too much handling	1. Stop handling
	2. Increased stress	2. Cover cage; house singly
	3. Temperature is too low	3. Raise temperature
	4. Parasitic or bacterial infection	4. Deworm; see veterinarian
	5. Foreign body obstruction	5. See veterinarian
	6. Tumor	6. See veterinarian
Wandering (Excessive)	1. Cage is too small	1. Increase cage size
	2. Hide box is too small or inappropriate	2. Change hide box size, shape, opening
	3. Cage is too hot	3. Lower temperature
	4. Hunger	4. Provide food
	5. Thirst	5. Provide water
	6. Mate searching	6. Mate or wait
	X. Whatever the cause	X. Use smooth top to protect snout
Seizures, Tremors, Star Gazing, Weakness, Paralysis	1. Vitamin B1 deficiency	1. Vitamin B1 injection; see vet.
	2. Septicemia (bacteria in blood)	2. Antibiotics; see veterinarian
	3. Encephalitis	3. See veterinarian
	4. Toxicity	4. See veterinarian
	5. Parasite migration	5. See veterinarian
Unusual Swelling	1. Steatitis (infl. of fat)	1. See veterinarian
	2. Cellulitis (infl. of tissue)	2. See veterinarian
	3. Tumor	3. See veterinarian
	4. Gravid	4. Prepare for eggs or babies

Most Commonly Used Drugs in Snakes

Problem	Drug	Dose
Bacterial Infection		
	Amikacin 50 mg/ml	2.5 mg/kg (0.0227 ml/lb) IM every 72 hours (#)
	Enrofloxacin 23mg/ml	5 mg IM every 48 hours
	Chloramphenicol	50 mg/kg SC SID
	Ceftazidime	20 mg/kg IM every 72 hours
	Carbenicillin	400 mg/kg IM every 72 hours
	Trimethoprim Sulfa	30 mg/kg SC every 48 hours
Intestinal Parasitism		
Amoebiasis	Metronidazole (Flagyl®)	60-125 mg/kg* PO (+)
Coccidiosis	Sulfadimethoxine (Albon®)	90 mg/kg PO 1st day then 45mg/kg 4 days in a row
Nematodes (hooks, whips, rounds)	Ivermectin 10 mg/ml	0.2 mg/kg (0.01) ml/1b (+)
	Fenbendazole 100 mg/ml	50-100 mg/kg (23-46 ml/lb) (+)
Cestodes and Trematodes (tapes and flukes)	Praziquantel 56.8 mg/ml	7.5-30 mg/kg (3-14 mg/lb) (+)
Cryptosporidia	None Effective (limited success with trimethoprim)	Formalin and Glutaraldehyde sufficient as disinfectants
External Parasitism		
Acariasis (mites and ticks)	Ivermectin 10 mg/ml	0.01 ml/lb PO or SC or IM (+)
	DDVP pest strips (Vapona)	One in. sq./10 gal. encl. for 5 days; place on top of screen (+)
	5% Sevin dust	Dust pillowcase and put snake in for 2-24 hours; dust cage also
Key to Symbols	(#) = 3–5 treatments, usually • *Lampropeltis and Drymarchon species should not be given more than 100 mg/kg; 40 mg/kg has been effective • (+) = Repeat in two weeks • IM = Intramuscular injection • PO = By mouth • SC = Subcutaneous injection • SID = Once per day	

The following three charts contain the doses of some of the drugs listed on this chart, calculated to the hundredth of a milliliter for the weight of the snake in question in the first column and the dose calculated by the metabolic scaling technique in the second column. For very small snakes, the necessary dilutions (with sterile water) of the standard drug concentrations are listed.

Small Snake Antibiotic Chart I
Amikacin Sulfate 50 mg/ml

Snake Weight (grams/pounds)	Dilution	Dose (ml)#	Dilution	At 37° C* Metabolic Scale Dose	Timing (every ___ hours)
5 g	1/100	.0.025 +	1/10	0.023	21
10 g / 0.02 lbs	1/100	0.050	1/10	0.038	25
15 g / 0.03 lbs	1/100	0.075	1/10	0.052	28
20 g / 0.05 lbs	1/10	0.010	1/10	0.064	30
30 g / 0.07 lbs	1/10	0.015	1/10	0.087	33
40 g / 0.09 lbs	1/10	0.020	1/10	0.108	36
50 g / 0.11 lbs	1/10	0.025	1/10	0.127	38
100 g / 0.22 lbs	1/10	0.050	1/10	0.214	44
200 g / 0.44 lbs	None	0.010	None	0.036	53
300 g / 0.66 lbs	None	0.015	None	0.048	59
400 g / 0.88 lbs	None	0.020	None	0.060	63
500 g / 1.1 lbs	None	0.025	None	0.072	67
600 g / 1.3 lbs	None	0.030	None	0.082	70
700 g / 1.5 lbs	None	0.035	None	0.092	73
800 g / 1.8 lbs	None	0.040	None	0.102	75
900 g / 2.0 lbs	None	0.045	None	0.112	77
1000 g / 2.2 lbs	None	0.050	None	0.120	79
1200 g / 2.6 lbs	None	0.060	None	0.138	83
1500 g / 3.3 lbs	None	0.075	None	0.164	88
1800 g / 3.9 lbs	None	0.090	None	0.187	92
2000 g /4.4 lbs	None	0.100	None	0.203	94
2300 g / 5.0 lbs	None	0.115	None	0.225	98

Recommended dose from literature is 2.5 mg/kg given IM every 72 hours. A loading dose (first dose) of 5.0 mg/kg is also recommended. IM=Intramuscular injection.

* 37° C is very hot for a snake. One would be advised to keep a snake warm, but not quite this warm, unless it is slowly adjusted to this temperature.

+ We have calculated doses one digit beyond the accuracy of the common smallest syringes (0.5 and 1.0 syringes). Round off to the nearest hundredth of a cubic centimeter (cc).

Small Snake Antibiotic Chart II
Baytril (enrofloxacin) 23 mg/ml

Snake Weight (grams/pounds)	Dilution	Dose (ml)#	At 37° C* Metabolic Scale Dose	Timing (every ___ hours)
5 g	1/10	.0.01	0.01	21
10 g / 0.02 lbs	1/10	0.02	0.022	25
15 g / 0.03 lbs	1/10	0.03	0.028	28
20 g / 0.05 lbs	1/10	0.04	0.034	30
30 g / 0.07 lbs	1/10	0.06	0.048	33
40 g / 0.09 lbs	1/10	0.09	0.058	36
50 g / 0.11 lbs	1/10	0.11 (.01)	0.070	38
100 g / 0.22 lbs	1/10	0.22 (.02)	0.118	45
150 g / 0.33 lbs	1/10	0.33 (.03)	0.160	50
200 g / 0.44 lbs	None	0.04	0.020	53
250 g / 0.55 lbs	None	0.05	0.024	56
300 g / 0.66 lbs	None	0.06	0.028	59
350 g / 0.77 lbs	None	0.08	0.030	61
400 g / 0.88 lbs	None	0.09	0.034	63
450 g / .99 lbs	None	0.10	0.036	65
500 g / 1.1 lbs	None	0.11	0.040	67
600 g / 1.3 lbs	None	0.13	0.046	70
700 g / 1.5 lbs	None	0.15	0.050	73
800 g / 1.8 lbs	None	0.17	0.056	75
900 g / 2.0 lbs	None	0.20	0.062	77
1000 g / 2.2 lbs	None	0.22	0.066	79
1500 g / 3.3 lbs	None	0.33	0.090	88
2000 g /4.4 lbs	None	0.44	0.112	94

\# Recommended dose from literature is 5 mg/kg given IM every 48 hours. A loading dose (first dose) of 5.0 mg/kg is also recommended. IM=Intramuscular injection.

* 37° C is very hot for a snake. One would be advised to keep a snake warm, but not quite this warm, unless it is slowly adjusted to this temperature.

Small Snake Antibiotic Chart III
Gentocin Sulfate 50 mg/ml

Snake Weight (grams/pounds)	Dilution	Dose (ml)#	At 37° C* Metabolic Scale Dose	Timing (every ___ hours)
10 g / 0.02 lbs	1/100	0.050	0.16	25
20 g / 0.05 lbs	1/100	0.100	0.28	30
30 g / 0.07 lbs	1/100	0.150	0.38	33
40 g / 0.09 lbs	1/10	0.020	0.047	36
50 g / 0.11 lbs	1/10	0.025	0.056	38
100 g / 0.22 lbs	1/10	0.050	0.094	45
200 g / 0.40 lbs	1/10	0.100	0.158	53
300 g / 0.70 lbs	None	0.015	0.021	59
400 g / 0.90 lbs	None	0.020	0.026	63
500 g / 1.1 lbs	None	0.025	0.032	67
600 g / 1.3 lbs	None	0.030	0.036	70
700 g / 1.5 lbs	None	0.035	0.040	73
800 g / 1.8 lbs	None	0.040	0.045	75
900 g / 2.0 lbs	None	0.045	0.048	77
1000 g / 2.2 lbs	None	0.050	0.053	79
1500 g / 3.3 lbs	None	0.075	0.072	88
2000 g /4.4 lbs	None	0.100	0.089	94

Recommended dose from literature is 2.5 mg/kg given IM every 72 hours. A loading dose (first dose) of 5.0 mg/kg is also recommended. IM=Intramuscular injection.

* 37° C is very hot for a snake. One would be advised to keep a snake warm, but not quite this warm, unless it is slowly adjusted to this temperature.

Large Snake Antibiotic Chart

Drug	Ceftazidime	Amikacin	Piperacillin	Chloramphenicol
Concentration	100 mg/ml	50 mg/ml	200 mg/ml	100 mg/ml
Dose	20 mg/kg	2.5 mg/kg	80 mg/kg	50 mg/kg
Snake Weight	Dosage	Dosage	Dosage	Dosage
4.5 kg/10 lbs	0.9 ml	.23 ml	1.8 ml	2.25 ml
9.1 kg/20 lbs	1.8 ml	.46 ml	3.6 ml	4.5 ml
13.6 kg/30 lbs	2.72 ml	.68 ml	5.44+ ml	6.9+ ml
18.2 kg/40 lbs	3.64 ml	.91 ml		9.1+ ml
22.7 kg/50 lbs	4.54 ml	1.14 ml		
27.2 kg/60 lbs	5.44 ml	1.36 ml		
31.8 kg/70 lbs	6.36+ ml	1.59 ml		
36.4 kg/80 lbs	7.28+ ml	1.82 ml		
40.9 kg/90 lbs		2.04 ml		
45.4 kg/100 lbs		2.27 ml		
68.1 kg/150 lbs		3.41 ml		
90.8 kg/200 lbs		4.54 ml		
Dosage Interval	Every 72 hours x5 to 7	Every 72 hours x5 to 7	Every 72 hours x5 to 7	Every 24 hours x10 to 14
Injection Site	IM*	IM*	IM*	SC or IM*

* Injection should usually be given in the front half of body.

+ certain drugs become impractical for large reptiles because of the large amount needed.

A hoading dose of 5 mg/kg is recommended, i.e. double the first dose.

Deworming Chart			
Drug	Fenbendazole	Praziquantel	Ivermectin
Concentration	100 mg/ml	57 mg/ml	10 mg/ml
Dose	50 mg/kg	20 mg/kg	.2 mg/kg
Snake Weight	**Dosage**	**Dosage**	**Dosage**
.45 kg/1 lbs	.23 ml	.16 ml	.01 ml
.90 kg/2 lbs	.45 ml	.32 ml	.02 ml
1.36 kg/3 lbs	.65 ml	.48 ml	.03 ml
1.80 kg/4 lbs	.90 ml	.64 ml	.04 ml
2.27 kg/5 lbs	1.14 ml	.80 ml	.05 ml
3.18 kg/7 lbs	1.59 ml	1.12 ml	.07 ml
4.09 kg/9 lbs	2.05 ml	1.44 ml	.09 ml
4.54 kg/10 lbs	2.27 ml	1.60 ml	.10 ml
6.81 kg/15 lbs	3.40 ml	2.40 ml	.15 ml
9.09 kg/20 lbs	4.54 ml	3.20 ml	.20 ml
11.36 kg/25 lbs	5.68 ml	4.00 ml	.25 ml
22.72 kg/50 lbs	11.36 ml	8.00* ml	.50 ml
45.45 kg/100 lbs	22.73 ml	8.00* ml	1.00 ml
Dosage Interval	Give once and repeat in two weeks	Give once and repeat in two weeks	Give once and repeat in two weeks
Route of Administration	Orally	IM	S.C., IM or Orally

* One should probably not exceed a dose of 8 ml at one time. A dose this large should be divided into 3 or 4 injection sites.
IM=Intramuscular injection.

Overheating

If a snake is frantically moving about its cage with its mouth open after being exposed to direct sunlight, or after being released from a transport device such as a pillowcase on a hot day, immediately get it out of the sun and immerse it in cool running water (except for its head, of course). This procedure has saved many a snake. Try to avoid having to resort to this measure by using proper transportation procedures. [See the section on *Transportation*.] The presence of a large bowl of water in the cage is the snake's first line of defense if the cage gets too hot. This is another common reason (aside from mites, preparation for shedding, or absence of a hide box) for snakes sitting in their water bowls for long periods of time. If you see your snake doing this, check to make sure the cage is not too hot and is well ventilated. The sunlight may be hitting the cage when you are not around; a heating pad may have been turned up by accident or may be malfunctioning. Similarly, if cages are stacked, the light from the cage below may make the cage above it dangerously warm.

After administering the cold-water treatment, you may wish to take your snake to a reptile-oriented veterinarian for an injection of a sterile electrolyte solution and possibly for a steroid injection. We have successfully used dexamethazone at a dose of five milligrams per kilogram of body weight intramuscularly (IM) twice per day for small snakes. Also, be aware that some snakes may be weak for days after an overheating incident; they will either recover slowly or die.

Parasites

EXTERNAL PARASITES

External parasites, most notably mites and ticks, can cause shedding problems, consume blood and cellular fluids, and possibly contribute to the spread of bacterial infections. It is important to note, however, that Ross and Marzec (1984) were unable to culture pathogenic bacteria from squash preparations of mites. Mites are also suspected of transmitting fungal, viral and blood parasite infections, but there is presently little evidence for this. Nevertheless, you should make every effort to keep mites out of your collection and eliminate them if they get started. Parasites can be treated at home, but remember that your veterinarian may be able to assist you tremendously in eliminating these pests. You may want to consult him or her immediately if you have a severe infestation of one specimen or if you have a large collection at risk. If you just have a few snakes or the outbreak is not too severe, you can usually attempt treatment and control of the parasites yourself. The snake may try to drown numerous parasites by soaking in the water dish for days on end. This behavior should alert you to the possibility of mites. The problem with the snake's attempt is that many of the mites will escape by migrating to the head, which the snake must keep out of the water in order

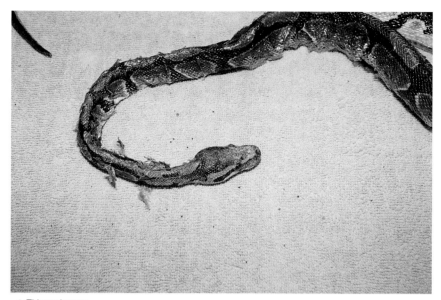

▲ *This snake was killed by mites.*

▲ *A mite viewed under a microscope.*

▲ *An adult tick.*

to breathe. The old treatment for mites, which made use of this behavior, included soaking the snake in soapy water and painting its head with various oils (such as olive oil or corn oil, *not* petroleum-based oils), while at the same time disinfecting the cage thoroughly. Dilute sodium hypochlorite solution (bleach at a concentration of one-to-three ounces per quart of water) works well as a cage disinfectant. Sevin® dust (five percent) has proven to be an extremely effective and safe way to eliminate mites, both in cages and on snakes (Levell, 1992). After cleaning and rinsing the cage, Levell advises sprinkling the powder liberally into the cage (up to 1/8 inch deep), letting it sit for several hours, and even placing the snake in with the powder for 24 hours. Mites are eliminated, and the snake appears unharmed. The cage and snake are then rinsed and dried, and the treatment is repeated two weeks later. Be aware that Sevin® dust treatment may be touchy, however, particularly if the snake is in shed at the time of treatment.

▲ *A tick in the eye socket of a ball python (Python regius). Ticks are common on some imported snakes. Ticks can be easily removed with forceps or tweezers. If present in large numbers, they can be eliminated by injecting the snake with ivermectin. The presence of ticks should be a signal to the owner that internal worms are likely present as well.*

Snake mites *Ophionyssus natricis* appear to the naked eye like small black beetles. Young mites and eggs are barely visible as small white specks. Generally speaking, they are usually spotted first in the water bowl because numerous adult mites drown there. Mites tend to congregate around a snake's eyes, where they cause periorbital swelling and a sunken-eye appearance. A wet cotton swab run around the rim of the eye will often collect several mites, which can be placed under a microscope to confirm the diagnosis.

Untreated wooden cages with large numbers of cracks and crevices are notoriously difficult to rid of mites. You probably have to paint or seal the wood or get rid of the cage. You should soak all items in the cage in the bleach solution, or bake them at 350° F (176.7° C) for 15 minutes, or throw them away. You must do this for all of the cages in the same room in some cases, or at least for all cages adjacent to those that are infested with mites. In many cases, the treatment with five percent Sevin® dust and a follow-up treatment two weeks later are all that are needed, but you may wish to try alternative measures to assure mite elimination.

One alternative is to place a piece of a Vapona®-laden strip (such as a No-Pest Strip®) in the cage. Some snake keepers have used flea collars such as Tech America Dog and Cat Flea Collars®, which contain approximately 1/2 and 1/4 the concentration of Vapona®, respectively, instead of No-Pest Strips® and can be used the in same way. We have used one inch of the strip for each ten gallons (approximately 40 liters) of aquarium space. Set the piece right on top of the aquarium screen. You can also put this piece in a small container (like a film container into which you have punched holes, and place it directly into the cage. The recommended method is to use the strip in or on the cage for five days (remove the water during this time), then remove the strip and put the water back into the cage. Fourteen days later, remove the water again and put the strip back in or on the cage for another five days. Afterward, wrap the strip in a plastic bag and save it for future use, as they may last for years if stored properly.

Note: Recently there has been some question as to the efficacy of Vapona®-laden strips. It appears that some mites may be developing a resistance to the active ingredient (Todd, 1983; Peterson and Orr, 1990). In addition, the safety of this product for some snakes has been questioned. Levell (1992) suggests that some members of the genus *Thamnophis* (garter snakes) appear to develop a "temporary paralysis," while Mader (1992) indicates that some pythons may show severe neurological signs when exposed to this insecticide. Indeed, we have noticed some degree of lethargy in garter snakes genus *Thamnophis* and water snakes genus *Nerodia* exposed to Vapona®, but we have never had any fatalities and still regard it as a fairly effective and safe product if used properly.

Avoid most mammalian flea powders or sprays; many of these organophosphate-based insecticides are toxic to reptiles. Some veterinarians and herpetoculturists have had a good deal of success with microencapsulated pyrethrin sprays (such as Sectrol House and Pet Flea Spray®), but others have reported some deaths (in young boas) when using these, so we urge caution when you use

▲ *Loss of coordination due to improper use of pest strip. Use with extreme caution for eliminating mites.*

these products. We have safely used the Sectrol Spray® on a variety of snakes, ranging from pythons genus *Python* to garter snakes genus *Thamnophis*, water snakes genus *Nerodia*, earth snakes genus *Virginia*, worm snakes genus *Carphophis*, and lined snakes genus *Tropidoclonion*. Two out of three Graham's crayfish snakes *(Regina grahamii)* demonstrated severe neurologic signs for several days after being sprayed with this product; thus, it is possible that these snakes are more sensitive to one of the ingredients in this spray than most other snakes. Other members of the genus are known to have very permeable skin, which may be a factor in their apparent sensitivity. Both of the snakes affected were either shedding or near a shed, while the unaffected snake was not, and both affected snakes recovered fully within several days.

Other sprays that recently have been recommended by reptile-oriented veterinarians include homemade mixtures of ivermectin and water or trichlorfon and water. The ivermectin spray can be mixed at a rate of a one-half

▲ Eye infection in a
rainbow boa.

milliliter of Ivomec® per liter (roughly one quart) of water
(Abrahams, 1992), and the trichlorfon spray can be mixed
at a rate of 8 milliliters of the eight-percent stock solution
(Trichlorfon Pour On®) per 400 milliliters of water (Boyer
and Boyer, 1992).

It is imperative to clean the cage, however, regardless
of what method you are using! If you can't disinfect cage
furniture thoroughly (a large piece of wood, for example),

Boyer suggests that it is not advisable to treat opaque
(close to shedding) snakes with the trichlorfon spray.
Perhaps snake skin becomes more permeable at this time,
so you may wish to avoid spraying snakes with most anti-
mite preparations during this part of their ecdysis cycle.
Your veterinarian can administer an injection of
ivermectin (Ivomec®) at a dose of 0.2 milligrams per
kilogram of body weight (which equals roughly 0.1
miligram per pound, which is 0.01 cubic centimeter per
pound if using the undiluted ten miligram per milliliter
solution). This will usually kill all of the mites and ticks as
well as many of the internal parasites with only two doses
given two weeks apart.

It is imperative to clean the cage, however, regardless
of what method you are using! If you can't disinfect cage
furniture thoroughly (a large piece of wood, for example),

throw it away and replace it. Remember: anything brought in from outside *must* be completely disinfected (either by chemical or physical means). Failure to do so may be the reason for the first outbreak of mites you experienced.

New snakes are the number-one cause of mite outbreaks. *All* new snakes should be quarantined for one to three months and examined regularly during this time for the presence of mites. In this way, an established collection is protected from these pests, which can spread rapidly from cage to cage.

Food items, even domestic mice raised in outdoor enclosures or around other snakes, are commonly a source of mites or other infectious organisms. For this reason, the purchase of "clean" mice is also an important factor in parasite control. Controlling parasites is even more difficult if you are maintaining a snake that you are feeding non-domestic food items, such as wild-caught lizards, snakes, birds, or mammals, even though freezing these items helps to reduce the possibility of a mite infestation.

INTERNAL PARASITES

Like most other animals, snakes may have internal parasites such as worms, which they usually acquire by ingesting food items that act as intermediate hosts. Some parasites enter the snake's body by penetrating its skin, whereas others are ingested with soil in infrequently cleaned cages. Snakes also can be infected by protozoan parasites. Most of the worms and many of the protozoan pests can now be safely treated, provided that they are detected early enough. Basically, snakes get similar kinds of worms as dogs and cats in terms of the kinds of damage that they do, their life history, and even the appearance of their eggs. These are hookworms, roundworms, whipworms, and tapeworms. Thus, it is not surprising to find that many of these worms respond to the same medications that are used for treating their canine and feline counterparts: fenbendazole (Panacur®), ivermectin (Ivomec®), and praziquantel (Droncit®), among others.

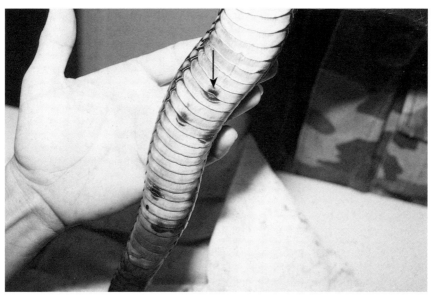

▲ *Fungal infection (ring worm) in an Indigo snake. A veterinarian needs to perform a fungal culture to be sure however.*

Ivermectin will kill some ophidian roundworms, whipworms, and hookworms; praziquantel will kill tapeworms and trematodes (flukes). Fenbendazole is an extremely useful and safe agent for eliminating roundworms, whipworms, hookworms, and probably many tapeworms. It appears to be more effective than ivermectin in eliminating worms that are commonly found in ball pythons *(Python regius)* (Klingenberg, 1992). We have found it especially useful in small snakes, in which cases ivermectin can be very dangerous, or in very heavily parasitized snakes such as those recently captured, when using ivermectin can also be risky. We will often treat the snakes with fenbendazole first and follow up with ivermectin later.

The most common protozoan parasites to infect snakes are amoeba and coccidia. Amoeba can be treated with metronidazole (Flagyl®) while coccidia can be treated with sulfadimethoxine (Albon®, Bactrovet®). [The doses for all of these drugs are listed in the drug chart.] Although you should make every effort to identify the parasites present by microscopic examination of the feces before

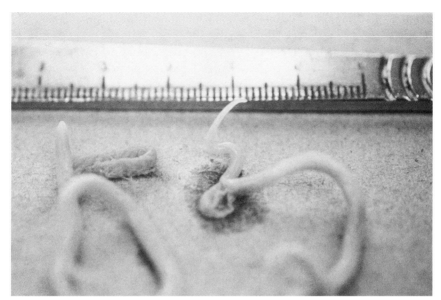

▲ Larval pentastomid worms are difficult to treat and contagious to people. It pays to have fecal exams done by a veterinarian.

treating the snakes, it is not a bad idea to combine a routine deworming of new snakes with a quarantine period before admitting them into a room with an established collection. The routine deworming should include the use of ivermectin and praziquantel for snakes that are likely to have tapeworms. They include those that consume fish, amphibians, or reptiles—such as hognose snakes genus *Heterodon,* indigo snakes genus *Drymarchon,* kingsnakes genus *Lampropeltis,* coral snakes genus *Micrurus,* and cobras family Elapidae.

Fenbendazole alone is a suitable substance for routine deworming, but it will probably not get all of the tapeworms, so you may want to reserve it for relatively "clean" snakes or very small snakes. If you want to be sure, bring a fecal sample to a reptile-oriented veterinarian and ask him or her to do a worm check for you. Any worms can be identified (at least into a major category), and protozoans may be detected. The veterinarian can then advise you on what medications to use and their correct doses, or treat them properly and safely for you. Most veterinarians will recommend that the snake be

▲ *Worms under a microscope.* Photo by Don Swerida, D.V.M.

examined and carefully weighed before dispensing or administering any medications. This is the way it should be done in most cases. [See chapter on *Medicines*].

Caution: There are some parasites in snakes for which there is *no* effective treatment at the time of this writing. This means that the only way to protect your snakes from these parasites is through a good quarantine program and the use of management practices that prevent the spread of parasites from one cage to another.

Pediatrics and the Pediatric Environment
(Perinatology)

Many herpetoculturists are now experiencing tremendous success in the captive propagation of numerous kinds of snakes, lizards, turtles, and crocodilians. These young animals may have specific environmental and dietary needs that differ from those of their parents. They may also have medical problems that differ from those of their elders. Fortunately, as herpetoculture has become more advanced, observations on the care and medical problems of neonate (newborn) snakes have increased dramatically; on the basis of these experiences, we can make some recommendations.

Birth/Hatching

In general, all neonates are subject to injuries to the umbilicus during the first several hours to days after live birth or hatching. In captivity, young snakes are particularly susceptible to evisceration (gutting) if their umbilical cord becomes stuck to a nonporous surface such as glass, which can happen as the snake rests. When the snake moves later, the dried umbilical cord may pull the yolk sac and other viscera through the umbilicus, resulting in sudden death or fatal peritonitis. With these young snakes,

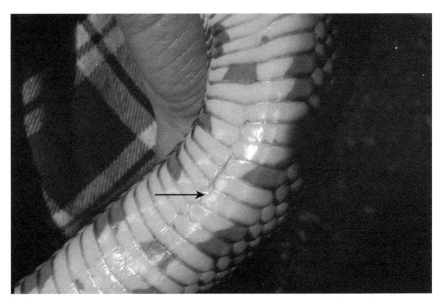

a substrate such as vermiculite or perlite (as used in the incubation box) or artificial turf usually works well until the umbilical cord dries out, which may take several days.

Feeding/Diet

After the initial period has passed, the young snakes will usually refuse to feed until they have shed for the first time, digested the rest of the yolk they have absorbed, or both. This process may take several hours in the case of very small snakes such as baby garter snakes, ribbon snakes genus *Thamnophis*, brown snakes or redbelly snakes *genus Storeria,*; it can take weeks in the case of larger snakes such as pythons genus *Python,* boas genus *Constrictor,* indigo snakes genus *Drymarchon,* or pine snakes genus *Pituophis.*

Young snakes may have dietary preferences that are very different from those of their parents. Most notable differences occur among the colubrids, especially kingsnakes genus *Lampropeltis,* glossy snakes genus *Arizona,* longnose snakes genus *Rhinocheilus,* night snakes genus *Hypsiglena,* crayfish snakes genus *Regina,* and Australian pythons genus *Liasis.* We are all too familiar with the juvenile gray-banded kingsnake *(L. alterna)*, which has no interest at all in pink mice (less than one week old) but will readily take lizards. The same can be said for most juveniles of the aforementioned snakes. Indeed, there may be numerous other subtle differences between the dietary preferences and requirements of neonate and adult snakes. Fortunately, the young of most commonly maintained species of snakes will thrive on a diet consisting only of domestic mice of varying sizes.

Smaller snakes have a number of other problems related to food and feeding. Generally, smaller animals have a higher metabolic rate. And even though reptiles are said to have indeterminate growth (they grow throughout their entire lives), they grow most rapidly during their first several years. Their small size also commonly limits the size of the meals they can consume and their body fat reserves. Consequently, they generally require more frequent feeding than adults if they are to grow or even to maintain themselves.

Physical Environment

Smaller animals possess a higher surface-to-volume ratio than larger animals. This means that they are more prone to desiccation (drying out) and overheating than their larger parents. Areas of high humidity and lower temperature within their cages are usually beneficial. A humidity box is one such area. Humidity boxes are plastic boxes that contain a moisture-retaining medium such as sphagnum moss. Aside from preventing desiccation, these boxes are also very useful in preventing dysecdysis (difficult shedding) in young and old snakes alike. We also have found these high-humidity shelters to be very important for adults of the smaller snake species (Rossi, 1992).

All of the other commonly accepted basics of herpetoculture, including cleanliness, temperature gradient, clean water, good ventilation, proper substrate, and provision of some kind of shelter still apply, although modifications to accommodate the smaller size of the neonates may be necessary.

▲ *Snakes that are subjected to overheating will often be seen with their mouths agape.*

Competitive Environment

When all of the dietary and environmental requirements are taken into consideration, competition among the neonates may be devastating. Siblings housed together may compete directly with each other for food, basking sites, or areas of appropriate humidity. Overt aggression is also likely in some species but should not be regarded as the major indicator of competition among young snakes.

What appears to be a cozy pile of siblings sitting in a corner or basking on a log may be comparable to a group of people in a lifeboat! It is a collection of individuals that are artificially packed together under the most stressful conditions and held together because they are surrounded by a more hostile environment. Their presence in close quarters may increase their stress to the point that neither their immune systems nor their digestive systems can function properly, and some individuals may become sick.

Most young animals have relatively naive immune systems and poor body reserves as well. When juvenile snakes are kept in close contact, any disease of an infectious nature may spread rapidly among them and will more likely result in a higher rate of illness and death than

It is strongly recommended that you house neonates singly.

it would among a similarly kept group of adults. We therefore recommend *strongly* that you house neonates singly if at all possible. In most cases, for example, it would be far better to house two neonate snakes in two five-gallon vivaria than it would be to house those same two snakes in one ten-gallon vivarium, assuming that there was sufficient space in the smaller enclosures. It is for this reason that snake breeders have been successful using plastic shoe boxes to house their young snakes. Even though the young snakes do not have much room, they *are* housed alone.

Personal Hygiene and Quarantine

Like other animals, snakes may harbor bacteria or parasites that may be contagious to their owners, as well as to other snakes in their collections. We therefore advise you to exercise some caution when handling or cleaning up after these animals. Keep new arrivals isolated from those established in a collection for a period of one to three months, generally referred to as the quarantine period.

PERSONAL HYGIENE

The first and perhaps the most important thing that you can do is to maintain good personal hygiene. Any time you handle a snake or any other animal, you *must* wash your hands thoroughly, preferably with a good antibacterial soap. Even if you use regular hand soap, the physical act of washing will in itself remove many potential pathogenic organisms. Liquid soap dispensers are better than bar soap, on which bacteria can survive.

Never eat or drink anything after handling a snake without first washing your hands. Never smoke a pipe, cigarette, or cigar after handling a snake without first washing your hands. If you use pens, pencils, or books around snakes, you should also consider them as potential sources of infection. Indeed, you should regard even doorknobs in snake rooms as contaminated, and you

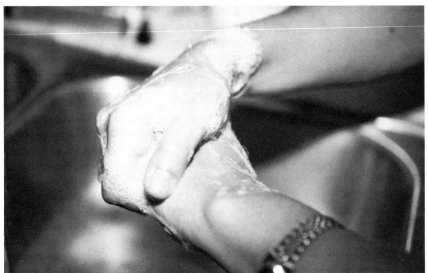

▲ *Washing hands with a good antibacterial soap will help to prevent the spread of diseases to the keeper and other snakes in a collection.*

should wash your hands after touching such areas. Be careful not to rub your eyes after handling a snake without first washing your hands, and remember that the same rules apply for the handling of snake food items, especially rodents and amphibians. Grier and others (1993) suggest that reptiles may be used in classroom situations with small children but that hand-washing is mandatory after *any* contact. Anyone with wounds or abrasions on his hands is well advised to cover both hands with disposable latex gloves prior to handling snakes.

If possible, do *not* use a kitchen sink—or any sink where dishes are washed or food is prepared—for cleaning snake cages or cage accessories, including water bowls. If you use a bathroom sink or tub, make sure to disinfect them thoroughly after each use, before they are used for other purposes. Refrigerators and freezers housing food intended for human consumption are not appropriate locations for the storage of frozen rodents, amphibians, or snakes. Although freezing may kill some parasites, it will not kill all of the potential parasites in these animals. Kitchen counters and other areas used for preparing food for people should also be off limits for reptiles and their food items, cages, and accessories.

Do not let a snake have free run of the house. Instead, confine it to a cage or a specific section of the house, and exercise caution when working in this area.

Make sure to encourage good hygienic practices in any children who live in homes where snakes are kept. Keep toddlers and snakes well apart unless an adult is present to wash the child's hands thoroughly after contact with the snake. Young children, the elderly, and immuno-compromised individuals (those with impaired or weakened immune systems) are especially at risk from some of the bacteria and parasites carried by snakes, so we recommend very strict sanitation procedures—or even total avoidance—in these cases.

Find a veterinarian who is familiar with snakes. Your veterinarian should perform a physical exam and repeated fecal exams on every snake you have. Fecal cultures taken to check for potentially communicable bacteria are also advisable in some cases, particularly when small children or immuno-compromised individuals are involved. These diagnostic tests may detect, and allow the treatment of, organisms that could affect the keeper and the snake, thereby protecting you both. Some diseases, pentastomiasis and salmonellosis for example, are either not treatable or not advisable to treat at this time. The diagnosis of such diseases, which have a real potential to transfer from snakes to people, is often regarded as grounds for the euthanasia of these animals. Should a snake in your care die, a necropsy (autopsy) should be performed in order to determine whether a potentially communicable disease was responsible.

Experienced reptile veterinarians will also advise you on the proper housing and diet of your snakes, thereby keeping them healthy and less likely to experience bacterial, fungal, or protozoal diseases. It also reduces the likelihood that you, the owner, will be affected. Cage cleanliness and disinfection are critical for the maintenance of healthy snakes and the minimizing of disease transmission. Household bleach diluted to a solution of three to ten percent is an excellent disinfectant that is inexpensive and widely available. There are numerous commercial disinfectants, but they vary in effectiveness and toxicity. There is no single disinfectant that can eliminate every disease-causing organism equally well.

Use of the correct diet alone (captive-born and captive-raised rodents or insects instead of wild-caught prey items) will tremendously reduce the risk of parasitism in snakes and thereby in the keeper. Freezing your snake's food items such as rodents and other small animals for storage purposes has some advantages. Numerous internal and external parasites will be killed, thereby reducing the risk of human and pet snake infection, but as this technique will not kill all parasites, it should be regarded as only partially effective. You should still treat these food items as if they may be harboring pathogenic organisms.

As a concerned keeper, you can also reduce the risk of contracting parasites from your animals by purchasing captive-born and captive-raised snakes. Doing this does not eliminate risks entirely, but it usually reduces the likelihood that a particular animal is heavily infected by parasites, especially by those parasites that require an intermediate host.

Terrestrial snakes are often less heavily infected than aquatic snakes, and their captive environments are less likely to harbor quite as large a variety of potentially disease-causing organisms. Consequently you may choose to minimize risk by choosing a terrestrial snake. In general, temperate species of snakes are less heavily infested than tropical species, although there are exceptions. Therefore, if you choose wild-caught animals, selecting those from temperate zones may reduce the risk of infestation somewhat.

The source of a purchased snake may have an influence on its pathogenic organisms. Those that have been housed in crowded cages at wholesalers and pet shops are more likely to have been exposed to these disease-causing organisms than those that have been purchased from a private breeder. You can reduce the risk of being infected by purchasing from a clean and reputable source.

QUARANTINE

Newly acquired or obviously sick animals should be treated with the utmost caution. Check them *extremely* carefully for signs of mite or other parasites when they arrive. [See the section on *Transportation*.] You should separate newly acquired snakes from any other animals you own and *always* work with them last. Never move instruments, water bowls, or uneaten food items from one cage to another. Use paper towels and dispose of them after each use, rather than using cleaning rags, which could inadvertently be used from one cage to another, spreading pathogenic organisms along the way.

You should keep your new snakes isolated from other established snakes for as many as three months while you observe them for medical problems. Observation includes repeated fecal exams to check for internal parasites such as *Cryptosporidia* or *Entamoeba*, which could be devastating to an established collection. You should eliminate all parasites (as much as possible) before allowing the snakes out of quarantine. A snake diagnosed with *Cryptosporidia* should *never* be allowed into a collection.

Visitors to a collection of snakes, or even those handling one snake for the first time, should be warned of a potential risk and asked to wash their hands after handling them. Do not give young children any reptile souvenirs, such as shed skins, scutes, or rattles, which could harbor *Salmonella* (Grier and others, 1993).

Psychological Factors

As we have pointed out before, stress reduction, disease prevention, and even treatment are intricately tied to creating the proper captive environment. The physical elements of this captive environment include proper heating, lighting, water availability, humidity, ventilation, and substrate. You should research the details of these elements for your pet's particular species. Although often ignored, psychological and social factors also play important roles in the keeping of healthy captive snakes. These factors include handling, visual stimulation caused by human activity, the presence or absence of cagemates, prey size and type (live or dead), hiding places, and cage stability.

You must restrict handling, and even the visual stimulation of nearby human activity, of especially nervous animals. Covering the front of the cage with construction paper or cloth with only small holes in it will usually reduce escape behavior significantly. Placing the snake's cage in a low-traffic area is also beneficial.

Whether or not to handle a snake is a decision that you must make on an individual basis. Young, fast-growing snakes (including most snakes intended for captive breeding) are best held infrequently, as they may regurgitate when stressed by handling. Some animals may appear to enjoy handling, while others become extremely nervous under the same circumstances. The presence of a cagemate may have a major impact upon the behavior of a snake. Commonly, one cagemate becomes dominant and the other submissive. The dominant one thermoregulates properly and stays healthy while the submissive one does not properly regulate its temperature and often suffers enough stress that it becomes sick. Indeed, the best way to house most captive snakes is to keep them singly.

Always try offering dead food items first. This method has been tremendously successful in inducing feeding in recently captured snakes. Apparently, a dead food item is far less intimidating to most snakes, and because many snakes are scavengers in nature, they will usually consume pre-killed rodents readily.

Providing a place in which the snake can hide is very important. This shelter, commonly referred to as a "hide box," appears to be one of the most critical pieces of equipment in any snake's cage. It has been suggested that these boxes provide the security needed to improve appetite, digestion, and breeding behavior, as well as to reduce the likelihood of vomiting. Perhaps they increase the life span of some captive snakes by years.

Frequent vibrations that a snake may experience if its cage is placed on an unstable shelf may increase stress, thereby causing a loss of appetite. This long-term exposure to vibrations may possibly contribute to the demise of some animals.

AGGRESSION IN CAPTIVE SNAKES

Novice keepers commonly wonder why a snake suddenly becomes aggressive. The term *aggression* as we use it includes striking, biting, and constricting, and it may be directed either at a cagemate or at the keeper. Other actions, including vibration of the tail (whether or not the tail possesses a rattle), hissing, puffing up, close-mouthed striking, and playing dead, are not usually regarded as acts of aggression in snakes, even though they may be preludes to aggressive behavior. Descriptions of some of the most common reasons for aggression in captive reptiles follow.

Hunger/Misdirected Feeding

A hungry snake will sometimes attack either a cagemate or its keeper. This misdirected feeding behavior is commonly caused by olfactory or visual stimuli. The most common example is the snake keeper who has just handled a rodent and then attempts to handle a snake. The snake, smelling the rodent on the warm hand, may confuse the hand with prey and, naturally, strike it.

Competitive Feeding Behavior

Two snakes housed in the same cage may compete for food in a very aggressive manner. This behavior is referred to in wild animals as interference competition and may definitely be a factor in a captive environment. Tugs of war over food items are common in cages with many natricine snakes (water snakes and garter snakes). In fact, the close quarters are likely to magnify these kinds of interactions.

Territoriality

Territories are believed to be areas guarded by animals because of the food, cover, basking sites, breeding places, or laying places they provide. Territorial disputes can become a common cause of aggression in captive reptiles. Recent studies have shown that snakes may be very territorial (Franz, 1992). Although aggression toward another member of the same species rarely has been observed in captive colubrid snakes, it is common in captive pythons (Ross, 1990). Some herpetoculturists have observed fighting in indigo snakes genus *Drymarchon* housed in the same cage.

Sexuality

Recently, there have been a number of reports of aggression by adult male iguanas against their female owners at certain times during the owner's menstrual cycle (Frye, et al. 1991). These reports suggest that the adult iguanas are responding to olfactory cues and are demonstrating displaced sexual aggressiveness. This kind of behavior has not been observed in snakes, but it is possible.

Inadvertent and Improper Training

Improper training can turn even a timid snake into an aggressive captive. We know of one snake keeper who always used to take her pet snake out of its cage, put in a live rat, then place the snake back in the cage. After several months of this routine, her timid snake bit her on the lip, arms, and elsewhere whenever she picked it up. The snake persisted in this behavior for months, and the owner was nearly ready to get rid of her pet, when someone suggested that she reverse the process: feed the snake heavily while it was in the cage, wait several days, then, wearing appropriate protection, pick up the snake. Basically, the keeper had trained her snake to look for food when she picked it up, so when it found none, the snake became aggressive. Some authorities have suggested that once snakes are established, you should feed them in cages that are separate from the cages in which they are normally maintained, thereby avoiding such problems. This kind of behavior may be difficult to reverse.

Pain and Irritation (medical problems)

Pain and irritation in snakes are caused by things such as internal or external parasites, irritating substrate, trauma, or a tumor. Pain brought on by parasites, toxins, or trauma may provide sufficient irritation to cause aggressive behavior. Typically, snakes agitated by such noxious stimuli will bite with far less provocation than snakes less irritated. We have seen very sudden onsets of aggressive behavior in snakes after they were infected with mites or certain protozoan parasites. The time of shedding is also frequently associated with increased irritability in snakes.

Normal Wild Response/Self-defense/Fear

1.   **Improper restraint:** Some species are naturally aggressive. Many snakes, including venomous ones, may bite in self-defense. To state that snakes may bite out of fear would be a supposition, but sometimes they become aggressive when cornered, trapped, or restrained, and no other alternative is available. Quick movement on the part of a handler sometimes seems to frighten snakes, and indeed this may be the case. Standing nervously in front of a snake for a long period of time while working up the

nerve to pick it up also tends to upset some snakes. Firm restraint about the middle of a snake's body will often elicit a bite.

2. Pseudo-release: Snakes living nonaggressively in captivity for years may suddenly become aggressive when they are placed either outside or in a different cage for a short period of time. Many owners have been bitten viciously by long-term captives that had previously never bitten, after the snakes have spent only a few minutes sitting outside on the ground. This kind of behavior may be related to a number of factors, such as different lighting or temperature, but we suspect that these animals may "think" that they are wild again, and respond as they would in nature to the approach of a large animal. We refer to this behavior as pseudo-release aggression because it occurs in snakes that otherwise are nonaggressive.

3. Juvenile defensive behavior/hyperdefensive response: Juveniles of most snakes appear to be particularly irritable and snappy, and generally they do not seem to tolerate much handing. Certainly, apart from any learned behavior, the survival instincts of juveniles favor escape and avoidance because most young snakes are subject to attack by predators in the wild. In nature, when a juvenile snake is picked up, it is about to become dinner, not adored or purchased. For this reason, many young snakes may be very aggressive, but they usually mellow out with age, as they learn that their keepers mean them no harm. For lack of a better name, this has been referred to as the juvenile hyperdefensive response. Do not assume that all these young animals will remain aggressive indefinitely.

Overcrowding Irritation

Snakes crowded into a small area may be agitated constantly by physical contact with other animals. This constant irritation may cause increased aggressive behavior, especially in more nervous individuals.

Sudden Temperature Changes

Elevations of ambient temperatures are known to affect the behavior of some snakes. Snakes handled relatively peacefully at room temperature may become extremely aggressive and bite repeatedly after they have been warmed up. In most cases, the aggressive behavior noted at the higher temperature is more likely to be the normal behavior pattern, while the apparently "peaceful" animal is one artificially subdued because of the lower temperature. At very high temperatures, aggressive animals may become lethargic again, giving the appearance of nonaggressiveness. When cooled off sometime later, their behavior may revert.

Summary

The causes of aggressive behavior in captive snakes are numerous. Improper handling techniques (rapid movement, excessive restraint) and improper husbandry practices (overcrowding) may increase aggressive tendencies, whereas the proper practices may reduce them in many, but not all, cases. We do not wish to overgeneralize about the innate aggressive tendencies of an entire species, but we encourage you to be aware that there are individual differences among snakes, just as there are among mammals. Much of this behavior may be learned, but some is innate. The widely held belief among herpetoculturists that captive snakes have individual personalities may have a basis in fact. The study of captive reptile psychology is as young as is herpetoculture, and we still have much to learn.

Medical problems certainly need to be considered in many cases of snake aggression. Your reptile-oriented veterinarian may be able to assist you in "unexplainable" cases of aggression.

Psychological factors affecting captive snakes are numerous. The nature of the animal itself plays a large part in how the snake adapts. Still, you need to be aware of some of the underlying factors that create stress in a captive snake and make every effort to minimize their effect. To do so, you must begin at the time of capture. Successful herpetoculture involves every phase of captivity, from transportation through housing and daily management.

Reproductive Failure/Dystocia

A particularly frustrating event in the life of a herpetoculturist is the persistent failure of the snakes in his or her care to reproduce. There are many reasons why this failure may occur, and fortunately, there also are a number of solutions.

The reasons for failure to reproduce are numerous and complex, but here we will simplify them by dividing them into three categories. These are: pre-mating problems, mating problems, and post-mating problems.

Pre-mating problems involve environmental factors such as cage size, lighting, temperature gradients, humidity, diet, and hibernation techniques. The age and overall health of your snake are also important in determining whether or not it will mate and be able to produce viable offspring. Animals that are not well adapted to captivity, or are in poor condition for reasons such as parasitism or previous overbreeding, are not likely to produce viable eggs or sperm. Improper temperatures (too hot *or* too cold) for too long, or the proper temperature for too short a time, are well-known causes of infertility in snakes of both sexes. In order to provide the proper temperature, humidity, diet, and so forth, you must research your species of snake, and in some cases you will learn through trial and error.

The mating process itself usually depends upon those factors previously discussed, and upon the environmental cues present at the time of the mating. Temperature, humidity, barometric pressure, cage complexity, and time of day may be critical in determining whether or not mating will occur. In order to mate, recently captured animals may require much more complex environmental cues than long-term captives (Ross and Marzec, 1990). Because every animal is an individual, any snake may be incompatible with another. Another factor is the social or behavioral environment. Some species require the presence of multiple males or females in order to mate consistently in captivity. Specific olfactory, visual, and tactile cues certainly play a major part in successful mating behavior, even though olfactory and tactile cues seem to be far more important than visual cues in many of the snakes studied to date (Gillingham, 1987).

Finally, previous trauma to, or infection of, the caudal spine or reproductive system (often unknown to the present owner) may severely hinder any reproductive effort. One good example is a fracture of the spine near the cloacal region of a snake, which prevents the proper alignment of its cloaca with its partner during attempted copulation. Such individuals may attempt mating for days without success.

Note: There should be a thermal gradient available in every cage because males and females may choose different temperatures at certain times for different functions.

Once mating has occurred, fertilization of the ova is possible, yet it is not definite. Consequently, timing is critical for many temperate-zone or so-called seasonal snakes, and you should make every effort to "synchronize" the pairs in your care by cycling them through the same temperature and photoperiod regime. [See Seigel and others (1987).]

Assuming that viable eggs and sperm were produced and that copulation occurred at the appropriate time, there are still a number of things that can, and frequently do, go wrong. Poor nutritional status, invasion by parasites, stress, frequent handling, inappropriate temperature gradient, or infection can cause a female to be infertile or partially infertile. Radiation (as in an x-ray), toxins (including some antibiotics), and trauma can also affect fertility in both sexes. In smaller species of live-bearing snakes, stress, especially in the form of handling, may cause spontaneous abortions.

Within a species, clutch size and weight of the young are directly correlated with the weight of the female, even though the weight of the young and clutch size are often inversely related to each other; in other words, the greater the number of young produced, the smaller the size of each. [See Siegel and others (1987).] Thus, there is a theoretical body mass below which a female cannot reproduce, or else can produce only very sickly young. Breeding a female with poor body mass may seriously compromise her life.

The retained products of a previous reproductive effort in certain female snakes can prevent the normal development of otherwise healthy embryos. Dystocia (inability to deliver eggs or live young, once they are produced) is certainly a common malady of oviparous and ovoviviparous snakes (those whose eggs develop after being laid, and those whose eggs develop within the maternal body, respectively). Lack of a proper laying place and lack of exercise are frequently to blame for this problem, but improper nutrition and inbreeding are also commonly the cause. [See the discussion on dystocia below and the section on *Egg Care*.]

If the young survive the initial stages of development, there is still a risk of death or deformity during the later stages. In oviparous species, the risk of death and deformity during incubation is significant. Desiccation, overhydration, lack of oxygen, exposure to temperatures too high or low, fungal infection, and predation by fly larvae are all common causes for the destruction of embryos within the egg. The proper incubation techniques and temperatures are discussed in this book's section on care of the eggs. You may need to research further for specific information on your snake's species.

Once you have worked out all of the intricacies of male and female husbandry, you should avoid some of the all-too-common traps of modern herpetoculture. These include pushing animals to breed when they are very young, inducing females to produce more than one clutch in a breeding season, and inbreeding generation after generation. Inbreeding may be especially devastating to young females, the most frequent victims of dystocia (slow or difficult labor or delivery). Klingenberg (1991) refers to these young obese animals as "lumps" and suggests that their poor muscle tone, a result of overbreeding, is a major cause of their dystocia.

The herpetoculturist must remember that reproduction is a luxury for captive snakes. Only if all of the animal's other needs are met will they reproduce successfully. Only if there is excess energy available to your snake will some of it be channeled into a successful and healthy reproductive effort, yet some emaciated snakes will breed, much to their detriment. You must first make every effort to maintain the snakes in question successfully, and then work on breeding. We are dismayed when we see the poor condition of so-called breeders presented to us by inexperienced herpetoculturists. Breeder snakes should be in peak physical condition, of the proper age and size, and kept in the appropriate environment. If these conditions are met, successful reproduction is almost inevitable. Problems arise and failures occur only rarely under such circumstances. The biggest problem, then, is trying to determine just what the appropriate environment is. We cannot overemphasize that environmental factors play a crucial role in all categories of mating problems, and in almost every facet of maintenance as well.

Dystocia or "Egg Binding"

As we discussed in the section on breeding, dystocia (difficulty in or failure to lay eggs or deliver young) is frequently related to an improper environment: inadequate temperatures, lack of privacy, improper laying medium, any handling, and such. Other causes include age and size, muscle tone, obesity, large egg size, infections, improper nutrition, parasites, structural defects (torsion of uterus, ruptured uterus or prolapsed uterus), tumors, and dehydration. [See the section on egg care for more detailed information on how to prepare a snake and her environment for successful egg deposition.] If dystocia or egg binding occurs, however, you should regard it as a medical emergency that must be treated within a few days (the sooner the better).

How do you know when a snake is egg bound? A snake may be egg bound if any of the following conditions apply.

1.   If she has failed to deliver her eggs by the end of the normal gestation period for her species. Because this period varies greatly as a result of a number of environmental factors, many herpetoculturists assume that a snake is egg bound if she has not laid her eggs by two weeks after the pre-laying shed, rather than after a set gestation period.

2.   If she has started laying and then stopped abruptly while still containing eggs.

3.   If she is straining, appears irritable or agitated, and has one or more eggs stuck at her vent for more than three hours. Under these circumstances, consider the following measures: (a) if no ventral heat is provided, add some; (b) make sure that the snake has a suitable private place in which to lay eggs, such as an egg-laying box; (c) be sure to provide drinking water, and (d) consider temporarily raising the humidity in your snake's enclosure. If these measure fail, warm water soaks or enemas are the next steps and the least invasive treatment techniques.

The following procedures should be performed *only* by an experienced reptile veterinarian. One of the first steps that many veterinarians take is to administer an injection of calcium. Brown and Martin (1990) recommend a flat dose of 50 milligrams of calcium gluconate intramuscularly, which may be repeated several times, while Lloyd (1992) suggests a dose of 2 to 5 milligrams per kilogram of body weight intramuscularly or subcutaneously of Calphosan® (10 milligrams per milliliter). We routinely use Calphosan® (calcium glycerophosphate) for this purpose. The rationale is that undernourished snakes may have a calcium deficiency and therefore have poor muscle tone. Finally, if these measures do not result in the passage of eggs, you should consider chemical induction.

Induction of the egg-laying process in snakes has taken a major step forward with the use of vasotocin rather than oxytocin. Certainly, oxytocin at a dose of two units per 100 grams has been effective in some cases, but there also have been many cases in which it was not.

▲ *Dystocia (egg binding) is an emergency. Medical induction or surgery is needed immediately. Make sure a suitable laying place is available, and raise the temperature and humidity in the meantime.* Photo by Steve Barten, D.V.M.

Because vasotocin is so much more effective, it has rapidly become the agent of choice for induction of egg laying in egg-bound snakes. Lloyd (1992) suggests a dose of 0.01 to 1 milligram per kilogram of body weight intraperitoneally. The problem is that vasotocin is an experimental drug that is not widely available at this time. If this procedure is unsuccessful, a prudent next step is ovocentesis of the caudal-most egg (inserting a needle into the egg nearest the cloaca and aspirating its contents) and repeating the dose of vasotocin or oxytocin. Note: The ovocentesis procedure is not without risk, and as Mader (1989) points out, it can cause the death of that embryo if it is viable (bound eggs are almost never viable) and can result in peritonitis (an infection in the abdominal cavity of the female) if it allows material from the egg to leak into the cavity. Mader also warns against this procedure being carried out in a nonsterile manner; the actual insertion of the needle may result in a lethal bacterial infection. Therefore, this procedure should avoided unless it is

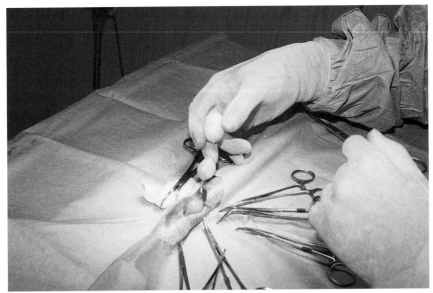

▲ Surgery was performed to remove the retained eggs.

absolutely necessary, and sterile technique *must* be used if it is attempted. Scrub the area to be perforated with a povidone iodine scrub, then wipe with alcohol several times before inserting a sterile needle. A 22-gauge needle on a 6- or 12-cc syringe is usually sufficient for this purpose. It is important to note, however, that the use of oxytocin or vasotocin can be fatal if the cause of dystocia is a blockage. The female overstrains. Many veterinarians advise against its use until all other causes have been eliminated.

Once the caudalmost egg is perforated and its contents removed, a gentle manual expression may deliver it from the uterus. If not, do *not* force the egg, or severe irreversible damage may occur, resulting in the death of the female or her inability to reproduce in the future. Klingenberg (1991) advises against manipulation of the drained egg, suggesting instead that the snake should be placed back in its cage and left alone while the calcium and oxytocin (or vasotocin) are allowed to work. We believe that if the egg is up high, this is appropriate, but if it is near the cloaca, then gentle and careful manipulation of the egg is acceptable. Manipulating a perforated egg may increase the risk of leakage of its contents, but then again, so will inefficient uterine contractions, and over a longer time. If the egg is delivered, place the snake back into the appropriate environment and let the calcium and vasotocin work on the rest of the eggs before attempting any more manipulation. If the female fails to lay eggs within 12 hours of this procedure, surgery is advisable. Antibiotics also are always advisable after ovocentesis and before surgery.

Good medical and surgical intervention may save a snake, but the *best* medicine, as we have emphasized throughout this book, is prevention through proper husbandry.

Respiratory Problems

Early respiratory signs, such as sneezing or a mild hissing noise, may signify a respiratory infection, although this is not necessarily the case. A chemical irritant such as that found in cedar shavings and cigarette smoke, high ammonia levels in dirty cages, or an allergen such as the dust on corncob litter may produce mild sinusitis, with consequent respiratory signs. In other words, there may be no infection to treat, only an environment to correct. Swelling of the head region and skin around the nares just prior to shedding may be accompanied by wheezing, and an agitated snake may produce sharp, short hissing noises. Because both of these observations may be mistaken for signs of a respiratory infection, you should observe your snake carefully after a shed, while it is at rest.

More serious and characteristic signs of a respiratory infection (although not specifically present *only* in respiratory infections) are open-mouth breathing, puffed-out throat, raised head, and increased mucus in the mouth, which results in bubble-blowing. Should a *bona fide* bacterial infection exist, bacteria may be secondary to another invader—like a fungus, parasite, or virus—or a compromised immune system has allowed a primarily bacterial infection in the absence of other invaders. The bacteria cultured from the trachea or oropharynx of these ill snakes are usually the same gram negative group which are cultured from the skin; therefore, the same approach is called for: environmental correction and supplemental heat are *always* indicated as the first steps in treating a suspected respiratory infection. If you see little improvement with these first steps, don't wait too long before getting that snake to a reptile-oriented veterinarian for initiation of antibiotic therapy.

Besides antibiotics, there have been several discoveries over the last few years that have improved a snake's chances of surviving a serious case of pneumonia. Boyer (1992) found that atropine at a dose of 0.02 to 0.04 milligrams per kilogram of body weight injected subcutaneously twice per day was much more successful when treating "moist pneumonias," and Qualls (1989) observed that Alupent® (metaproteranol sulfate), which is a bronchodilator, eases respirations when a concentration of 0.6 percent Alupent® is nebulized (administered as a fine mist) for ten minutes per treatment three times per day. Qualls also observed that one drop nebulized in a small amount of water would help to dry up mucus as well.

Several viruses have been associated with respiratory disease in snakes. Perhaps the most notorious viral infection of snakes is paramyxovirus, which has affected large numbers of viperid and elapid snakes in collections around the country. This virus usually causes acute pneumonia, as well as neurologic signs, and death within several days. Another virus that causes severe and chronic respiratory signs is the VEBS virus. VEBS stands for Viral Encephalitis of Boid Snakes, and it causes these respiratory signs in boas, whereas in pythons it causes progressive neurologic signs such as incoordination and weakness. The outcome of either infection is usually death. We suspect that there may be numerous other viral diseases in snakes that may not be quite as severe and from which most snakes recover; however, we do not know for certain. A viral infection may respond partially to increased environmental heat, as this will stimulate the snake's immune system, even though deadly viruses like paramyxovirus will require prompt and aggressive veterinary care if the snake is to have a fighting chance.

Fungal pneumonias occur more frequently than most herpetoculturists or reptile veterinarians would like to believe. They are commonly misdiagnosed as nonresponsive bacterial pneumonias, but they are treatable, although treatment is sometimes difficult or expensive. Desert snakes housed in plastic containers with poor ventilation seem especially prone to fungal pneumonias, but any snake housed in moist conditions for long is a prime candidate for a fungal infection. One western hooknose snake *(Gyalopion canum)*, having been housed in a plastic shoebox for two months, died with signs of respiratory problems, and a necropsy revealed fungal hyphae in the lung tissue. We have seen a number of wild snakes that have suspicious-looking lesions when they have been captured in low, wet areas or after weeks of very rainy weather. We have successfully applied amphotercin B in a nebulizer at the dose recommended by Jacobson (1988), which is 5 milligrams in 150 milliliters of saline solution nebulized for one hour twice per day for one week.

Although not as common as gastrointestinal parasites, lung parasites are commonly present and may be a source of significant damage to your snake's lungs. Perhaps the most common lung invaders are the nematodes of the genus *Rhabdias*. Fortunately, as part of their life cycle, their eggs and larvae are frequently shed in the snake's stool, even though the primary infection of *Rhabdias* is in the lung, thereby making a diagnosis easier. Unfortunately, neither the larvae of the genus *Rhabdias* nor that of *Strongyloides* can be readily distinguished in a stool smear. Your veterinarian can make a presumptive diagnosis by performing a tracheal wash or by reviewing the primary problem of the snake. A positive tracheal wash or a history of primarily respiratory signs would suggest *Rhabdias*, while a negative tracheal wash with a history of primarily gastrointestinal signs would suggest *Strongyloides*. The presence of any rhabditiform larvae (a term for the larvae of both genera) in the stool should be noted as such, and treatment should be initiated. No group of worms appears more widespread among captive snakes than the rhabditiform larvae. We have found this type of worm in more than 20 species of snake, ranging from South American cribos genus *Drymarchon* to African ball pythons *(Python regius)*, Asian reticulated pythons *(Python reticulatus)*, black striped snakes *(Coniophanes imperialis)* from southern Texas, Mexican rosy boas *(Lichanura trivirgata trivirgata)* from Arizona, and kingsnakes genus *Lampropeltis* from Florida. Hence, you should examine all snakes carefully and use the appropriate dewormer. Among these are ivermectin, fenbendazole, and levamisole at doses listed in the drug charts.

Pentastomids are another type of parasite that may occur in the lungs or under the skin. Diagnosis of these parasites is a very serious matter for two reasons: first, they are capable of infecting people; second, there is presently no known treatment for these worms, either in snakes or in people, except surgical removal. It is for this reason that many veterinarians suggest euthanasia for these snakes, once they spot the characteristic five hooked embryonated eggs during a fecal exam. Junge and Miller (1992) discuss respiratory diseases in reptiles and their treatment in more detail.

Seizures, Tremors, Incoordination, and Symptoms of Neurological Problems

Signs of neurological problems that we commonly observe in snakes include seizures, tremors, incoordination, weakness, "star gazing," blindness, and flaccid paralysis. In snakes, these signs usually are related to one of three things: infection, toxins, or a metabolic defect or deficiency. Trauma to the head or spine, and overheating may also result in neurological symptoms.

A severe infection that involves brain tissue or that produces toxins affecting the brain is the most likely reason for obvious neurological symptoms such as seizures, tremors, or incoordination. You should be especially suspicious if there also are other signs of infection such as pneumonia or mouth rot. Bacterial infections may respond to treatment, but viral and amoebic infections are difficult to treat. The VEBS virus causes such symptoms, and there is no effective treatment. Toxins

These snakes have had a seizure. Snakes have seizures for a number of reasons. An infection of the brain is the most likely cause.

such as those found in insecticides (including pest strips with Vapona®, if used improperly), paint, some medicines, and bacterial toxins may all cause signs of neurological disorder.

Lastly, fish-eating snakes are prone to thiamin (vitamin B1) deficiency. It may cause seizures in as little time as six months in snakes on a diet of fish alone, if the diet is not supplemented with a vitamin and mineral powder. A thiamin deficiency may be prevented by feeding your snake a varied diet, including fish-scented, pre-killed mice if possible, or placing a small piece of a Brewer's yeast tablet inside some of the pre-killed fish that you feed to your snake. Should your snake exhibit a tremendous increase in nervous behavior followed by seizures, administer between 0.05 and 0.1 cc of Tech America's Multi B Complex® intramuscularly. This drug usually halts the symptoms within a matter of hours. The treat-

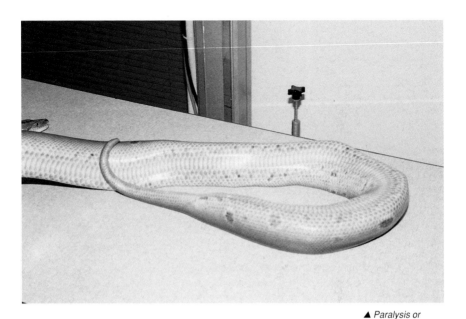

▲ Paralysis or paresis (weakness) often indicates severe toxicity or damage to spinal cord. This green Burmese (Python m. bivittatus) had fractured its spine.

ment and prognosis for recovery vary considerably with nerve problems. Bacterial infections may respond nicely to the appropriate antibiotics, while very few snakes will survive an amoebic or viral encephalitis.

To treat toxicity, you must remove the toxin, as well as the snake, from its immediate environment. Washing the snake with soap and water may help. Atropine®, at the dose listed in the respiratory section, may be helpful in cases of organophosphate toxicity. After this treatment, give the sick snake fluids and supplemental heat. Note that metronidazole and ivermectin both are capable of causing neurological symptoms if given at much higher than the recommended dose. Use paint and mite-control products with caution; make sure that snake cages are well ventilated and completely dry, and remove the water bowl for a little while after these products are applied. After painting or varnishing a cage and it is thoroughly

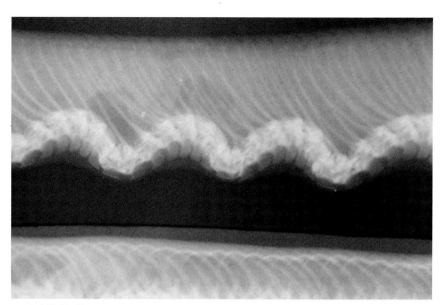

▲ *A Florida king snake with multiple pathological fractures from hematogenous spread of Proteus vulganis bacteria. X-rays reveal the seriousness of this infection.* Photo by Don Swerida, D.V.M.

dry, turn cage heating devices to high for a few days before introducing a snake; heat further drives off solvent fumes. Polyurethane in organic solvent is notorious for leaking more fumes after cage heat is turned on.

Stomatitis (Mouth Rot)

Infections of the mouth are so common in snakes that you should always examine a snake's mouth before purchasing it and as part of a routine examination to ascertain a snake's health. Abnormal closure of a snake's mouth might be the first clue that something is not right. Small red spots of hemorrhage (called petechiations by veterinarians) may be the second clue that an infection is starting. These two signs may also occur immediately after a big meal, so this is not always the best time to examine a snake. Other reasons that they should not be examined after feeding include vomiting, which is more likely to occur if a snake is handled soon after it has eaten.

More definitive signs of infection are swelling, discoloration of the mouth, and a cheesy exudate (ooze) along the gumline. Advanced stomatitis may be accompanied by excessive mucus in the mouth; most likely this is a result of fluid coming from the trachea, which could indicate a case of pneumonia. Should the exudate be membrane-like and firmly attached to the lining of the mouth, it probably indicates membranous or diptheritic stomatitis, which is the most severe form of stomatitis and usually extremely difficult to cure.

▲ *This ball python has a severe case of mouth rot. Photo by* Don Swerida, D.V.M.

Untreated, even mild stomatitis can become severe within a period of days. As with all other kinds of infections, the first step in treating stomatitis is correcting the environment and supplementing the heat. After that, appropriate antibiotic therapy based upon a culture and sensitivity test is advisable. Gram-negative bacteria are most likely responsible, and antibiotics effective against gram-negative bacteria are the most logical choice of medication.

In addition to injectable antibiotic therapy, topical medication of the mouth is usually necessary. Topical povidone iodine solution works well in most cases, and hydrogen peroxide has also been useful in many cases. Some veterinarians combine these two products, believing that the hydrogen peroxide will help drive the povidone iodine (Betadine®) deeper into tissues, thereby making it more effective. Another topical that we have used with a great deal of success is Gentocin Opthalmic Solution® (Schering-Plough). Numerous other topical solutions have been tried with varying degrees of success, but in our experience, these three, or combinations of them, work very well.

Recently, chlorhexidine (Nolvasan® in two percent nonscented solution) diluted in 20 to 30 parts water has been used with excellent results as a topical for stomatitis (Suedemeyer, 1992). Suedemeyer stated that this solution is commonly effective against many strains of pseudomonas (bacteria). He suggests the inclusion of chlorhexidine discs on cultures and sensitivity tests. To administer any solution, gently open the mouth, and place several drops of it on the top and bottom of the snake's mouth once or twice per day, depending upon the severity of the stomatitis. Do this after removing any necrotic (dead) tissue. We gently restrain the snake, open the mouth with a blunt probe, and scrape out the material with a scalpel (#15 blade).

Sudden Death

The sudden death of an apparently healthy long-term captive is perhaps the most frustrating and puzzling event to snake keepers. There are a number of possible reasons, but only a necropsy (autopsy) will tell, and even it may not always provide a clear reason. [See the discussions on psychological factors and maladaptation.]

One of the most common causes of sudden death in a captive snake is a parasite that penetrates the intestine and thereby causes internal bleeding and peritonitis. In many cases, this can be avoided by a regular fecal exam and deworming program. Another cause of sudden death is dehydration or kidney failure. A snake kept too warm and dry, consistently without sufficient water available, may well die from uric acid buildup and eventual kidney damage. Past overdosage of certain antibiotics also can cause kidney failure. Overheating kills reptiles by denaturing enzymes and also by altering the metabolism in such a manner that life processes cannot continue. It also causes rapid dehydration. Malfunctioning heating devices or thermostats are often to blame, as are empty water bowls and the lack of a moisture box.

Heart disease is being uncovered as more common in captive snakes than was previously thought. Overfeeding, combined with a lack of exercise results in obesity, high cholesterol levels and increased risk of a fatty heart.

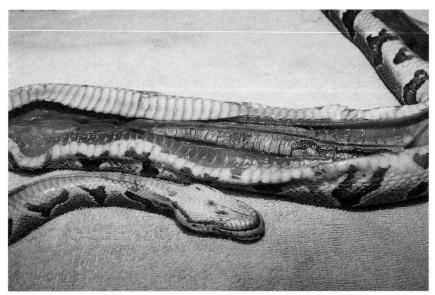

▲ *Python with "Brown spots." This snake died the next day. Necropsy revealed hemorrhagic septicemia.*

Smaller snakes are particularly susceptible to septicemia (high levels of bacteria in the blood), which although commonly undetected may develop and run its fatal course in a matter of days. This disease is frequently associated with filthy cage conditions. Larger snakes also are prone to septicemia, but the signs of infection may be more apparent.

Vitamin and mineral deficiencies may result in the acute appearance of neurological symptoms, even though the problem is usually caused by chronic malnourishment. The appearance of neurological symptoms in fish-eating snakes, caused by a vitamin B deficiency, is such an instance. [See the discussion on neurologic signs for more details.]

Long-term captives at one location may stop eating or die suddenly when switched to another location, even if ideal husbandry conditions exist. Typically, the reason for this situation is bacterial overgrowth in the gut, leading to gastroenteritis or septicemia; all are related to stress, which caused immune-system suppression. Veterinarians are generally leery about using antibiotics as a preventive measure, but in certain circumstances, as with new arrivals, snakes may benefit from a course of antibiotics indicated by a fecal culture. You should also make every effort to provide a stress-free and clean environment for all snakes, especially for new arrivals.

Sudden death immediately after brumation (hibernation) occurs in a similar manner. Some zoos have had massive die-offs of long-term captive snakes during such times. What appears to be happening is that the snake's immune response lags behind the rapid growth of pathogenic bacteria and protozoans, resulting in death usually within a week after the snake's emergence from hibernation. If a snake shows any signs of illness, health decline, or sluggish behavior following removal from hibernation, be prepared to administer metronidazole and amoxicillin orally, and possibly amikacin by injection (follow your veterinarian's instructions). The dosages of these drugs are listed in the drug chart at the end of the medicine section. This entire disease process can be prevented by performing fecal exams, and cultures and sensitivity tests, then treating the condition(s) accordingly, prior to transporting or hibernating *any* snake. Only healthy animals should be hibernated or shipped.

Transportation

Improper methods of transportation are among the major causes of disease and death among captive snakes. Failure to properly insulate the containers holding these reptiles may result in either overheating or a chill, each of which may lead to disastrous consequences. Five minutes in direct sunlight may be all it takes to kill a trapped snake, even a heat-loving diurnal snake, while a brief chill may result in fatal pneumonia.

Generally speaking, snakes are best transported in clean cloth sacks such as pillowcases. Place the snake in the pillowcase, along with crumpled newspapers to cushion it and protect it from trauma. Tie the neck of the pillowcase in a knot upon itself, having first made certain that the snake is *not* in the area about to be tied. Small snakes may benefit from the addition of shredded news-paper which has been misted with water, which helps keep them from becoming dehydrated. You may then place the bag inside a styrofoam container, into which you have punched several small holes. *Never* transport an uncontained reptile; such foolish practice has resulted in many automobile accidents!

For shipping purposes, place the styrofoam box inside a cardboard box, clearly marked with the destination address and, in large letters: "Live Animals/Avoid Extreme Heat or Cold." Punch a few small holes through

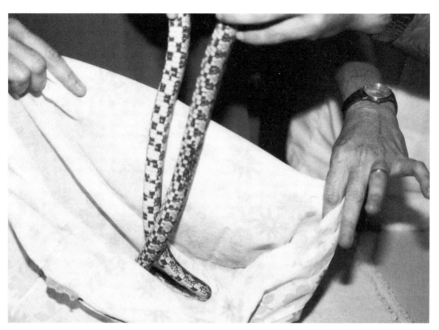

▲ *Snakes are best transported in clean cloth sacks such as a pillowcases as shown here.*

the cardboard box as well as the styrofoam container *before* placing the animals inside. Reptiles are best sent by Express Air Freight. Delta Air Lines has offered a reliable service for this purpose over the years. Venomous reptiles require additional packaging, usually double wooden, metal-rimmed crates. Contact your shipper for specific requirements.

Professional shippers frequently ship snakes and other reptiles at night during hot weather and during the day in cold weather, so that they are not likely to be exposed to temperature extremes. These professionals also make sure that they call before shipping to make that someone will be at the airport waiting for the package. This procedure shortens the duration of the snakes' crowded condition and may improve their chances of survival. Some shippers also enclose heat-producing packs (found in sporting goods stores) when shipping reptiles in the winter, and ice-containing plastic containers or cool-packs when shipping them in the summer.

You should place recently shipped snakes in their quarantine cages immediately upon receipt and offer them

▲ For safe shipping than place the bagged snake within a cushioned box as shown here, or preferably inside a foam box which is then placed inside the cardboard.

water. There is no telling how long these animals have been deprived of water, and several more hours may make a difference. Next, you should carefully examine them for mites or evidence of a respiratory infection. Even if you observe no signs of respiratory problems immediately, they may appear within several days if a chill has occurred, so be on the alert.

Snakes should be checked for mites as soon as they are unbagged. Some experienced reptile veterinarians advise putting a snake immediately into a shallow water soak for one to two hours. Follow with a soapy water soak, then rinse the snake thoroughly and place it in a quarantine cage. Another variation of this anti-mite treatment that we use regularly is to spray the snakes heavily with ivermectin and water spray [discussed in the section on *Parasites*.]

Dispose of the shipping crate and bags immediately. You may save the bags for future use, but *only* if you wash them with bleach, and you should do so as soon as possible to avoid the risk of a mite outbreak in a collection.

One last warning is in order. Coolers are generally no match for direct sunlight. Neither are tents, cars, or even houses in many cases. While driving with snakes in a car, you *must* keep them out of direct sunlight. A good safety precaution during a trip is to use a digital battery-operated indoor/outdoor thermometer with a probe to monitor the temperature in the box. This device has saved the lives of a number of snakes in the authors' care. The new Koolatrons® are superb devices for safely transporting snakes in a car.

Trauma
(Rodent Injuries, Escape Injuries)

Injuries are among the most common reasons that snakes are brought to veterinarians for treatment. The majority of these injuries fall into three major categories. The first and most common source of injuries is rodents. These occur when live rodents are left unattended in a snake's cage. The second group of injuries is usually observed in animals that have escaped; these are scratches, abrasions, splinters, or burns. The third group is usually the willful injury that occurs when an escaped snake is found by a neighbor who is unappreciative of snakes. All three types of injuries may be severe or even fatal. Yet they are all preventable!

You should *never* leave a live rodent unattended in a snake's cage for any length of time. Feeding it pre-killed rodents is an excellent way to prevent injury to your snake. Frozen rodents are now widely available and economical. The use of secure cages will prevent the other two types of injuries. Neodesha® reptile cages (Neodesha Plastics, Inc., Neodesha, Kansas) are nearly escape proof. They consist of a molded one-piece body and a tight-fitting, sliding front door. The lack of sharp corners and abrasive materials also reduces the likelihood of trauma within the cage.

Once an injury has occurred, you must evaluate the severity in order to determine the proper treatment. Almost all bite wounds and other open wounds are likely to become infected. Topical ointments such as Silvadene Cream®, Betadine®, and Polysporin® will usually work effectively, as we discuss in the section on dermatitis, but systemic (injectable) antibiotics are often necessary as well. The ointment you choose should be placed on the lesion once per day, and the wound may take several months to heal. Of course, any inadequacies in the environment and the diet of these animals need to be corrected, or all treatments will fail. Heavy feeding is advisable during this time to increase healing and to improve the immune response.

Crushing injuries, such as those caused when a cage lid falls on a snake or when a snake is run over by a vehicle, may respond to immediate fluids injected into the injured area. Not only do such injections restore the shape to the damaged area immediately, but they also improve

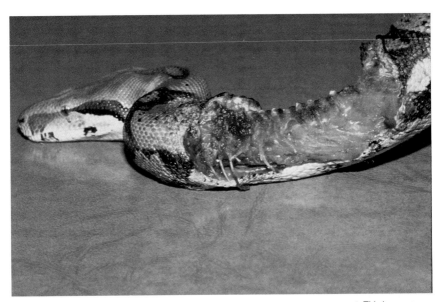

▲ *This boa was fatally injured by a ferret. It was impossible to save with this much trauma. House your snakes properly to prevent such injuries.* Photo by Steve Barten, D.V.M.

the circulation; we have seen snakes with severe injuries survive after being treated in this manner. Systemic, and sometimes oral, antibiotics are also warranted in these cases because there may be some damage to the gut. We recommend that you *not* feed the injured animal for several weeks following such trauma, and then only very small meals. A large meal may cause more trauma, possibly even reopening a small tear that was healing.

Skeletal or spinal injuries may also be present and can be severe in some cases. In many instances (both in the wild and in captivity), these will heal without any kind of treatment. In some cases, however, it may be necessary to repair this damage. Most veterinarians will need to radiograph (x-ray) such an animal to determine what kind of repair may be necessary or possible. Injuries of this type may even result in paralysis below the fracture when the spinal cord is severed. Snakes injured in this manner may survive and heal to some extent, even eventually developing a "spinal crawl," a reflex crawling that assists in locomotion. These snakes are unlikely candidates for breeding, however.

This snake has severe injuries from multiple mouse bites. Photo by Don Swerida, D.V.M.

Open wounds will usually heal by scarring over. A veterinarian may reduce this effect by suturing (applying stitches to) a clean, fresh wound. This needs to be done within several hours of the trauma taking place. If more time elapses, most veterinarians will consider the wound too contaminated to attempt closing it. Bite wounds are considered contaminated immediately and most veterinarians will not close such a wound.

Vomiting and Regurgitation

Another common reason that snakes are brought to veterinarians for exams is that they are regurgitating or vomiting. In mammals, it is generally quite easy to distinguish regurgitation from vomiting because regurgitation occurs soon after eating, while vomiting occurs hours or days after ingestion of food. Regurgitated food is generally undigested food expelled primarily (and passively) from the esophagus, whereas vomitus consists of partially digested food, usually actively expelled from the stomach. With reptiles, distinguishing between the two actions can sometimes be difficult. The point is that the snake is not holding down food, and possible causes are numerous.

There are ten common causes for vomiting or regurgitation in snakes, but you should remember that there may be more than one cause for any particular case. A good example of this has been termed "regurgitation syndrome" (Ross, 1990), which occurs in boid snakes and is known to have a number of possible causes .

Causes of Vomiting and Regurgitation in Snakes

1. Handling too much or too soon after feeding
2. A drop or sharp rise in ambient temperature or just improper ambient temperature for digestion

3. Increased stress (including mating) soon after feeding
4, A meal that is too large, too old, too toxic, or being offered too frequently
5. Bacterial infection
6. Protozoal infection (amoeba, coccidia, flagellates)
7. Metazoan (worm) infection
8. Tumor
9. Overdrinking right after eating
10. Underhydration

Handling a snake right after it has fed is asking for trouble. Wait at least two days, depending upon the size of the meal.

Sometimes, making cage changes, adding a new animal to the enclosure, or some other apparently minor change may be very stressful for a reptile and cause it to vomit its last meal. Perhaps the most common cause of vomiting or regurgitation is an ambient temperature that does not allow normal digestion. More frequently, a drop in ambient temperature is the cause of sudden onsets of vomiting or regurgitation, yet it also can be caused by sharp rises in temperature. This symptom should serve as a warning to the herpetoculturist that the normal ambient temperature may be marginal for digestion.

Very large meals may cause irritation of the gastrointestinal tract and result in vomiting or regurgitation. Very frequent feedings have the same effect. In snakes, irritation leading to vomiting or regurgitation may also result from swallowing a large meal backwards, because the spines of a fish or the fur of a mammal are generally directed backwards. Very old meals may be loaded with bacteria or bacterial toxins, which in some cases may induce vomiting or regurgitation, similar to people with food poisoning. Some food items, including certain frogs and toads, produce chemical toxins that may be a little more than some snakes can handle.

Bacteria flourish in a filthy environment; those that are extremely contagious are commonly discovered as the cause of outbreaks of vomiting. These bacteria may be responsible for an inflammation of the lining of the stomach and intestine known as bacterial gastroenteritis. Not surprisingly, two of the contagious gram-negative bacteria, *Salmonella* and *Arizona,* are frequent offenders. These bacterial infections are among the few cases in snake medicine in which oral antibiotics are deemed appropriate and necessary. We have successfully used Entromycin® at a dose of one teaspoon per kilogram of body weight every two days for one week, whereas Ross and Marzec (1984) and Ross (1990) have used ciprofloxacin and amoxicillin successfully.

As we discuss parasites, protozoan and metazoan, in some detail later in this section, we will not dwell upon them here. But you should always consult your veterinarian if you suspect parasites. It is usually a waste of time and money to pump one routine deworming agent after another into a debilitated snake without the benefit of repeated fecal exams or a gastric (stomach) wash and it may be dangerous for the snake as well.

A foreign-body obstruction commonly occurs in captive snakes that are housed on the improper substrate. Check your references and use the proper substrates. Towels, handcloths or T-shirts are *not* acceptable because they have been ingested by accident! Incidentally, you can sometimes induce the vomiting of an ingested towel or handcloth by causing an ambient temperature drop. Give the snake a sterile electrolyte solution intraperitoneally to counteract the dehydrating action of the towel, and then place it in a relatively cool area, about 50 to 60° F (10 to 15° C). Vomiting of these soft objects usually occurs within two to three days under these circumstances. You must monitor the snake for dehydration, and intraperitoneal fluids and antibiotics are advisable during and after this procedure. Note that this is a practical "field approach," to be used when sedation and endoscopic retrieval of the handcloth are not possible for some reason. This approach is definitely worth considering before attempting surgical retrieval, but you must carefully monitor the state of hydration in these animals.

In older snakes which are becoming more common as a result of improved care, tumors are definitely a possibile cause of regurgitation or vomiting. Your reptile-oriented veterinarian can determine if one is present, by means of palpation or with a radiograph.

Many snakes tend to drink heavily after gorging on a large meal. Sometimes, it appears that they may over-drink; vomiting or regurgitation occurs soon afterwards.

Underhydration theoretically causes irritation to the lining of the gut by blocking the smooth passage of food because of the increased friction and thereby increasing the likelihood of vomiting or regurgitation. When vomiting occurs, isolate the animal, restrict handling, raise the temperature if it is too low (or drop it if it is too high), feed less and/or smaller items, and make sure that the cage is clean and the food is fresh. If vomiting persists, have your snake examined by a reptile-oriented veterinarian, who may suggest a fecal exam, a culture and sensitivity test, or a biopsy, in order to determine the cause or causes of the problem and the proper treatment.

Weight Loss

Weight loss (or failure to gain) is another common complaint with captive snakes. As you might expect, parasites are high on the list of possible causes, but there are a number of other reasons this condition might occur, and some are not immediately obvious, assuming that the animal is eating.

POSSIBLE CAUSES OF WEIGHT LOSS

1. Insufficient amount of food offered

If a snake is housed singly in the proper environment and has a good appetite, yet loses weight in spite of this, your first approach may be to try the obvious: offer more food. If this does not work, it is time to consider the following possibilities listed here.

2. Parasites

The variety of parasites in reptiles is enormous, but basically they can be divided into two groups: (1) internal parasites, which include metazoans (worms) and protozoans (one-celled organisms such as amoebas, flagellates, and coccidia); and (2) external parasites such as mites and ticks. Most of these parasites are either known to be, or are strongly suspected of being, quite harmful to their hosts and should be eliminated by your veterinarian. [This procedure is discussed in some detail in the section on parasites.] In herbivorous reptiles, some one-celled organisms are commensals (harmless) or symbiotic (helpful to the host by aiding in the breakdown of food or in the production of vitamins), but this kind of parasitic interaction has not been determined in snakes (even though there is a possibility that intestinal bacteria contribute to the production of vitamin B1). Certainly, the presence of these organisms in an animal that is losing weight and that has less-than-normal stools should make you suspicious. Frequent fecal exams are important.

3.   Improper caloric content or poor digestibility of diet
Some foods are not very digestible. An insectivorous snake consuming a large percentage of beetles (and some of their larvae), mature crickets, and grasshoppers may be getting a large percentage of indigestible material, namely chitin, more than it would if it were eating soft-bodied insects, younger insects, or recently molted or metamorphosed insects.

4.   Maldigestion or malabsorbtion
It is quite possible that a snake may not have the ability to digest or absorb its food. This problem may relate to a defect in the pancreas or gastrointestinal tract. The atrophy of the pancreas in vipers is one example of this kind of problem. Another is the hypertrophy (thickening of the lining) of parts of the gastrointestinal tract when infected by *Cryptosporidia*.

5.   Increased metabolic rate caused by high environmental temperature
The metabolic rate in snakes rises with a rise in body temperature: therefore, the caloric requirement for maintenance will also most likely increase at higher body temperatures. A snake maintained in a room that is not air-conditioned will probably need nearly twice as much food as one in an air-conditioned room—at least during the summer in most areas of our country. Theoretically, there may be a high temperature range beyond which cool-climate snakes cannot eat sufficient quantities of food to maintain themselves when they are thus exposed for long periods of time, even if they are fed heavily. In fact, it has been suggested by some authorities that vitamin deficiencies may occur in some ectotherms when they are

maintained at high temperatures, because different metabolic pathways occur at different rates; at constantly high temperatures they may use up co-enzymes (vitamins) in one reaction faster than they can be replaced by another.

You can avoid temperature-related problems by researching the preferred daily and seasonal temperatures of your particular species and keeping your snakes as near as possible to those temperatures. An example is the Andean milk snake *(Lampropeltis triangulum andesiana)*, which lives in the wild at high elevations and requires lower ambient temperatures, 72 to 75° F (22.2 to 23.9° C). If such information on your species is not available, provide a temperature regime that is similar to the geographic area from which the animal originated. The use of thermal gradients within the enclosure is also important.

6. Metabolic rate elevated by endocrine disorder
Endocrine disorders such as primary hyperthyroidism, in which the thyroid gland is enlarged and secretes increased levels of thyroid hormone, may cause weight loss and dysecdysis (abnormal shedding). There are medications that may control this problem. We have successfully used methimazole at a dose of one milligram per kilogram of body weight per day for three weeks.

7, 8. Dehydration (acute and chronic) and kidney failure
Dehydration caused by a very dry environment and an improperly located water source can contribute to weight loss. Over time, kidney damage can result, which makes a snake unable to conserve body fluids and possibly lose protein through the urinary tract. For these reasons you should provide water regularly to most snakes. [See also the discussion on excess humidity in the section titled Disease Preventing Enclosures and Procedures.] In addition, high humidity refuges should be made available to some snakes.

9. Cancer cachexia (tumor-inhibited appetite, modified metabolism)
Tumors can cause weight loss because the substances they sometimes produce may inhibit feeding and change the metabolism. A regular checkup by your veterinarian may reveal suspicious masses, which in many cases can be successfully removed.

Although these are some of the most likely reasons for weight loss, anorexia (failure to feed) is by far the most common reason for weight loss in captive snakes. [See the discussion in the section titled *Anorexia and Inappetence*].

Choosing a Veterinarian

At the time of this writing, there are more than 50,000 veterinarians in the United States. The vast majority of them have received superb training in the medicine of domestic animals, but few have received much training in reptile medicine. Being a cross section of humanity, veterinarians on the whole are individuals who are not particularly fond of snakes. Indeed, the best reptile veterinarians were herpetologists first. They often are aware of the natural history of their patients and can advise their clients accordingly. Because more than 90 percent of reptile maladies are related to an improper captive environment, knowledge of such is critical to treating these animals properly. We wish that one of these knowledgeable individuals could live near every snake keeper because they would be the ideal choice. Unfortunately however, herpetologists-turned-veterinarians are rare, numbering perhaps less than 50 in the United States.

Another group of veterinarians who treat reptiles (a much larger group, but by no means a large one) consists of individuals with a definite interest in and respect for reptiles, and who have taken extra courses in reptile care. At least one of these caring and knowledgeable veterinarians can be found in most large cities; usually they will work with you in treating your snake's medical problems.

A third group of veterinarians are very caring and helpful individuals who know very little about reptiles but will agree to help you, perhaps because no other help is available in your area. They may candidly admit that they don't know much about snakes, but that they'll get their books out and work with you to help your pet. These individuals can benefit tremendously if you bring them a copy of this book.

The last group includes those who do not work on reptiles at all, and worse, those who will treat them without really knowing anything about their care. Fortunately, the latter situation rarely occurs.

Of course, you want to choose a veterinarian from one of the first three groups, ideally one of the first two. You can usually find the best reptile veterinarians by asking your neighbors, friends, local snake breeders, pet shops, zoos, museums, or veterinary school. Another excellent source of information is your local herpetological society. A national herpetological directory has been published, and it may be available from your local public library or herpetological society. The veterinarian you choose should have a clean, well-equipped office, and regular office hours with an appointment system, which usually creates reliable and relatively timely office visits.

Laboratory tests for snakes may include radiographs (x-rays), fecal exams, blood chemistry and complete blood counts, cultures and sensitivity tests, and tissue biopsies. Good reptile veterinarians usually handle the snakes gently and take extra precautions with species known to be somewhat aggressive. They may have snakes of their own, and they rarely show fear of snakes.

A good reptile veterinarian should do the following for your snake: (1) ask what the problem is and take a medical history; (2) perform a complete physical exam; (3) perform the tests necessary to confirm a diagnosis (these tests should be done discriminately); (4) encourage questions and discuss environmental or dietary corrections; (5) provide some literature; and (6) explain the fees. In the last 20 years, major strides have been made in reptile medicine. A great number of research papers and books has been published about the medical care of reptiles. Recently, a number of veterinarians formed the Association of Reptilian and Amphibian Veterinarians, a group dedicated to the dissemination of information relating to the medical care of these animals. At the time of this writing, there are around 1,000 members.

Because of these advances, knowledgeable veterinarians can be tremendously helpful in saving the lives of many sick snakes and increasing the growth rates and productivity of breeders, much as they do for many other species. Pet owners and professional breeders alike have discovered that veterinary fees are usually wise investments.

For Membership Information write to: Association of Reptilian and Amphibian Veterinarians Box 605 One Smithbridge Road Chester Heights, PA 19017

References

Abrahams, R. 1992. Ivermectin as a spray for snake mites. *Bulletin of the Association of Reptile and Amphibian Veterinarians.* 2(1): 8.

Boyer, T.H. 1992. Use of atropine for eliminating excessive mucus in Boids. *Bulletin of the Association of Reptile and Amphibian Veterinarians.* 2(1): 6-7.

Boyer, D., and T.H. Boyer. 1992. Trichlorfon spray for snake mites *Ophionyssus natricis. Bulletin of the Association of Reptile and Amphibian Veterinarians.* 1(1): 2-3.

Brown, C.W., and R.A. Martin. 1990. Dystocia in snakes. *The Compendium on Continuing Education/Small Animal.* 12(3): 361-368.

Cowan, D.F. 1980. Adaptation, maladaptation and disease. *Reproductive Biology and Disease of Captive Reptiles.* Ed. by Murphy and Collins. SSAR Contributions to Herpetology, 191-196.

Fitch, H.S. 1982. Resources of a Snake Community in Prairie-Woodland Habitat in Northeastern Kansas. *Herpetological Communities* (N.J. Scott, Jr., Ed.). U.S. Fish and Wildlife Service Wild L. Res. Rep. 13: 83-97.

Franz, R. 1992. Personal communication.

Frye, F.L. 1991. *Biomedical and Surgical Aspects of Captive Reptile Husbandry.* Vols. I and II. Krieger Pub. Co., Melbourne, Fl. 637 pp.

———., D.R. Mader, B.V. Centofanti. 1991. Interspecific (Lizard:human) sexual agression in captive iguanas *(Iguana iguana).* A preliminary compilation of eighteen cases. *Bulletin of the Association of Reptilian and Amphibian Veterinarians* 1:4-6, 1991.

Funk, R.S. 1992. Personal communication.

Gillingham, J.C. 1987. Social behavior. *Snakes: Ecology and Evolutionary Biology.* New York: McGraw Hill. Pp. 184-209.

Grier, J.W., M. S. Bjerke, and L.K. Nolan. 1993. Snakes and the Salmonella situation. *Bulletin of the Chicago Herpetological Society.* 28 (3): 53-59.

Hammack, S.H. 1991. New Concepts in Colubrid Egg Incubation: A Preliminary Report. *Fifteenth International Herpetological Symposium on Captive Propagation and Husbandry.* Ed. by Michael J. Uricheck. Pp. 103-108.

Jacobson, E.R. 1988. Use of chemotherapeutics in reptiles medicine. *Exotic Animals*. New York: Churchill Livingston. Pp. 35-48.

———. 1992. Reptile Dermatology. *Kirk's Current Veterinary Therapy XI. Small Animal Practice*. Ed. by Kirk and Bonagura. Philadelphia: W.B. Saunders. Pp. 1204-1210.

Jarchow, J.L. 1988. Hospital care of the reptile patient. *Exotic Animals*. New York: Churchill Livingston. Pp. 19-34.

Junge, R.E., and R.E. Miller. 1992. Reptile respiratory diseases. *Kirk's Current Veterinary Therapy. Vol. XI*. Pp. 1210-1213.

Klingenberg, R.J. 1991. Egg binding in colubrid snakes. *The Vivarium* 3 (2): 32-35.

———. 1992. A comparison of fenbendazole and ivermectin for the treatment of nematode parasites in ball pythons *Python regius*. *Bulletin of the Association of Reptile and Amphibian Veterinarians*. 2 (2): 5-6, 49.

Levell, J.P. 1992. Eradicating snake mites: A brief history with the report of another method. *Bulletin of the Chicago Herpetological Society*. 27 (10): 205-206.

Lloyd, M. 1992. Vasotocin: the reptilian alternative to oxytocin. *Bulletin of the Association of Reptile and Amphibian Veterinarians*. 2 (1): 5.

Mader, D.R. 1989. Egg retention in reptiles. *The Vivarium* 2 (5): 13-14, 23-24.

———. 1992. Personal communication.

———. 1993. Obesity in Reptiles. *Reptiles* 1(2): 33-35.

———, and K. DeRemer. 1992. Salmonellosis in Reptiles. *The Vivarium* 4 (4): 12-13, 22.

Paul-Murphy, J., D.R. Mader, N. Kock, and F.L. Frye. 1987. Necrosis of Esophageal and Gastric Mucosa in Snakes Given Oral Dioctyl Sodium Sulfosuccinate. *Proceedings of the American Association of Zoo Veterinarians*. pp. 474–477.

Peterson, K. H., and R. Orr. 1990. An unusual mite infestation at the Houston Zoo. *Bulletin of the Chicago Herpetological Society*. 25 (1): 10.

Qualls, J.M. 1989. A novel treatment for snake pneumonia. *The Vivarium* 2 (1): 12-13.

Regal, P.J. 1980. Temperature and light requirements of captive reptiles. *Reproductive Biology and Diseases of Captive Reptiles*. Ed. by Murphy and Collins. SSAR Contributions to Herpetology 1. Pp. 79-89.

Ross, R., and G. Marzec. 1984. *The Bacterial Diseases of Reptiles: Their Epidemiology, Control, Diagnosis and Treatment.* Inst. for Herp. Research. 114 pp.

———. 1990. The Reproductive Husbandry of Pythons and Boas. *Institute for Herpetological Research.* 270 pp.

———. 1990. Regurgitation Syndrome in Boid Snakes. *Thirteenth International Herpetoloical Symposium on Captive Propagation and Husbandry.* Ed. by M.J. Uricheck. Pp. 81-85.

Rossi, J.V. 1992. *Snakes of the United States and Canada.* Melbourne, Florida: Krieger Publishing Company. 210 pp.

Rossi, John. 1996. Dermatology in Reptile Medicine and Surgery (Mader Ed.) Saunders Publishing Co. Philadelphia. 512 pp.

———. and R. Rossi. 1995. *Snakes of the United States and Canada:Vol. II. Western Area.* Melbourne, Florida: Krieger Publishing Company.

Rosskopf, W.J. 1992. Silvadene cream as a topical medication. *Bulletin of the Association of Reptile and Amphibian Veterinarians.* (2) 1:6.

Sedgewick, C.J., A. Haskel, and M.A. Pokras. 1986. Scaling drug dosages for animals of diverse body sizes. *Wildlife Rehabilitation.* 5: 3-11.

Sedgewick, C.J., and M.A. Pokras. 1988. Extrapolating rational drug doses and treatment periods by allometric scaling. *Proceedings of the American Animal Hospital Association. 55th Annual Meeting.* Pp. 156-157.

Seigel, R.A., J. T. Collins, and S.S. Novak. 1987. *Snakes: Ecology and Evolutionary Biology.* New York: McGraw Hill. 529 pp.

———., and J.T. Collins. 1993. *Snakes: Ecology and Behavior.* New York: McGraw-Hill Inc. 414 pp.

Snider, A.T., and J.K. Bowler. 1992. Longevity of Reptiles and Amphibians in North American Collections. *Society for the Study of Amphibians and Reptiles* Circ. No. 21. 40 pp.

Suedemeyer, W.K. 1992. Use of chlorhexidine in the treatment of infectious stomatitis. *Bulletin of the Association of Reptile and Amphibian Veterinarians.* 2 (1): 6.

Todd, S. 1983. Vapona resistant mites? The Herptile. *Journal of the International Herpetological Society.* 8 (3): 90.

Index

A

Abscesses 22
anal gland 23-24
Acquiring 9
Adult 10
Age 11
Aggression 100
Amikacin sulfate 72
American Federation of
Herpetoculturists 16, 54
Anorexia 25
Antimicrobial
susceptibility report 68
Appearance 12

B

Baytril 73
Birth 89
Bites 132-134
Boids
relatively small 15
large species 16
very large species 16
Burns 33, 35

C

Caging 4
Cancer 141
Captive environment 3
Captive-born 10
Carrion flies 52
Cataracts 63
Causes of vomiting 135
Cleaning 7
Color pattern 12
Colubrids 13
Competitive
environment 92
feeding 101

Constipation 36
Cultures 68

D

Death
sudden 124
Dehydration 39, 141
Dermatitis 41
Deworming chart 76
Diarrhea 45
Diet 7, 26, 90, 140
Digestion 140
Disease 3, 4, 148
preventing enclosures 4
Disinfection 7
Disposition 10
Drug chart 71
Dysecdysis 47-48
Dystocia 105, 108, 110-111

E

Egg binding 108
Egg bare 49
Enclosures 4
Endocrine disorder 141
Environment
competitive 92
physical 91
Escape 53
injuries 131
management of 53
Escape injuries 131
Examination 17-18
External parasites 79

F

Fear 102
Feeding 90
behavior 101
frequency 57
Fractures
neck 54
Fungal infection 86

G

Gentocin sulfate 74
Geriatrics 61

H

Handling 17
Hatching 52, 89
Hide boxes 5
Humidity 5
Hunger 101
Hygiene 94
Hyperdefensive response
103

I

Identification 65
Import 10
Improper shedding 47
Inappetance 25
Incoordination 117
Internal parasites 85
Irritation 102

J

Juvenile defensive behavior
103

K

Kidney failure 141

L

Large snake antibiotic chart
75
Large species 16
Lighting 7

M

Malabsorbtion 140
Maladaptation 31
Maldigestion 140
Medical factors 28
Medicines 67
Metabolic rate 140, 141

Microchip
  anicare 66
Mites 80-81
Mouth rot 121-122

N

Natricine snakes 14
Nesting 49
Neurological problems 117
Not eating 25

O

Obesity 57, 60
Overcrowding 27, 103
Overheating 77

P

Pain 102
Paralysis 55, 119
Parasites 79, 85, 139
Pediatrics 89
Perinatology 89
Preventing 4
Problem/solution chart I 69
Problem /solution chart II 70
Psychological factors 27, 99

Q

Quarantine 94, 97-98

R

Regurgitation 135
Relatively small 15
Reproductive failure 105
Respiratory problems 113
Rodent injuries 131

S

Seizures 117-118
Selection 13
Self-defense 102
Sex 10
Sexuality 101
Shelters 5

Size 10
Skin
  color 44
  lesions 41
  splitting 42
  tearing 43
  texture 44
Small snake antiobiotic
  chart I 72
Small snake antiobiotic
  chart II 73
Small snake antiobiotic
  chart III 74
Snake 10, 13
  acquiring 9
  adult size 10
  age 11
  appearance 12
  captive-born 10
  handling 17
  import 10
  selection 13
Stomatitis 121
Substrate 5

T

Temperature changes 103
Territoriality 101
Thermal gradient 6
Thermometer 34
Tick 80-81
Training 102
Transportation 127
Trauma 131
Treatment 17, 21
Tremors 117

V

Venomous snakes 18
Ventilation 5
Very large species 16
Veterinarian 143
Vomiting 135

W

Weight loss 139
Wild response 102
Worms 87

Notes